MW01110413

Selected Letters of Mary Antin

Writing American Women
Carol A. Kolmerten, *Series Editor*

Mary Antin in 1926
Photograph courtesy of Rosemary Richards

For Fay

SELECTED LETTERS OF
Mary Antin

EDITED BY

EVELYN SALZ

Evelyn Salz
Aug. 25, 2000

SYRACUSE UNIVERSITY PRESS

Library of Congress Cataloging-in-Publication Data
Antin, Mary, 1881–1949.
[Correspondence. Selections]
Selected letters of Mary Antin / edited by Evelyn Salz.
p.   cm. — (Writing American women)
Includes bibliographical references (p.).
ISBN 0-8156-0607-9 (cloth : alk. paper)
1. Antin, Mary, 1881–1949 Correspondence.   2. Jews—United States
Correspondence.   3. Jews—United States Biography.   4. Jews—
Cultural assimilation—United States.   5. Immigrants—United States
Biography.   I. Salz, Evelyn.   II. Title.   III. Series.
E184.37.A58A4 1999
979'.04924'0092—dc21
[B]   99-3702

To my husband, Henry,
and my children, Heidi, Jonathan, and Talya

Evelyn Salz is the college archivist at Western New England College in Springfield, Massachusetts, and works as a reference librarian at Storrs Library in Longmeadow, Massachusetts. She published an article about Mary Antin in *American Jewish History* in 1996.

Contents

Illustrations

Editor's Acknowledgments

Gratitude goes first to Kathryn Ritzen who accompanied me on several "letter hunts," who read every word I wrote, and who provided me with much needed encouragement and good advice.

I am especially grateful to James Young, who "introduced" me to Mary Antin. Many thanks also to Jules Chametzky. Both University of Massachusetts professors encouraged me often throughout the writing of the book.

Special thanks go to Anne Ross, Mary Antin's granddaughter, who brought me into the family and introduced me to her mother, Josephine Ross, and to her sister, Rosemary Richards. I thank them for permission to reproduce the unpublished letters and for providing copies of treasured family photographs.

I am grateful to the Memorial Foundation for Jewish Culture for partial support in the publication of this book.

I would also like to thank Arthur Antin, Joyce Antler, Doris B. Gold, Fred W. Drake, A. Arthur Grabau, Oscar Handlin, Kathryn Hellerstein, Susan Koppelman, Henry J. Laskowsky, Keren McGinity, William McKee, Andrea Most, Ambassador Ronald E. Neumann, Liu Ruixun, Jonathan Sarna, Werner Sollors, and Sam Bass Warner, Jr., for their helpful suggestions.

To my fellow archivists: Kevin Proffitt at American Jewish Archives, Abigail H. Schoolman at the American Jewish Historical Society, Roberta Zhonghi and Eugene Zepp at the Rare Books and Manuscripts Department of the Boston Public Library, Mark N. Brown at Brown University, Rochelle Rubenstein at the Central Zionist Archives, Jean W. Ashton at Columbia University, David S. Zeidberg at the Huntington Library, Rabbi Mayer E. Rabinowitz at the Jewish Theological Seminary, Virginia Smith and William M. Fowler Jr. at the Massachusetts Historical Society,

Kathleen Nutter at the Sophia Smith Collection at Smith College, Michael Ridderbusch at West Virginia University Library, and William McKee, trustee at Gould Farm, thank you for providing copies of Mary Antin's unpublished letters and, wherever possible, for granting permission for the publication of the letters.

Permission to reprint the unpublished letters has been provided by American Jewish Archives (Horace M. Kallen Papers and Abraham Cronbach Correspondence); American Jewish Historical Society (Louis Lipsky Papers); courtesy of the Trustees of the Boston Public Library (Thomas A. Watson Papers and Warren Dale letter); Brown University Library (Maud Howe Elliott Papers); Central Zionist Archives (Israel Zangwill Papers); Rare Book and Manuscript Library, Columbia University (Randolph Bourne Papers); Gould Farm, courtesy of William McKee (Rose and Sydney McKee letters; Caroline Goodyear, Agnes Gould and Mildred Schlesinger letters); Huntington Library, San Marino, California (Mary Austin Papers); Library of the Jewish Theological Seminary of America Archive 96, Box 2 (Bernard G. Richards Papers); Massachusetts Historical Society (Ellery Sedgwick Papers); Ambassador Ronald E. Neumann (Ruth B. Woodsmall letters); and West Virginia University Library (Margaret Prescott Montague Papers).

In the preparation of this book, I have been ably aided by my copy editor, Annette Wenda.

Introduction

Theodore Roosevelt's declaration that "You are an American in whom I so deeply believe that I should be sorry if I could not include your photograph" was the pinnacle of Mary Antin's successful assimilation and recognition as a noted American autobiographer, political activist, and public figure. In 1913 the former president wrote her about including Antin's photograph as the portrait of an ideal American in his planned autobiography. She had come a long way from her impoverished youth and adolescence in Chelsea and Boston, Massachusetts. She had come even further from the poverty and anti-Semitism of the Pale of Settlement in Russia that forced the Antins, along with more than 2 million European Jews, to emigrate to the United States. In 1894, the thirteen-year-old Antin arrived in Boston with her mother and siblings to be reunited with her father who had preceded them three years earlier.

Today, Mary Antin is best known for her widely acclaimed autobiography, *The Promised Land,* which was published in 1912, and for some of her short stories, notably "Malinke's Atonement," published at about the same time. Although *The Promised Land* brought fame to Antin, she was also, in addition to being the first documenter in English of Russian Jewish life in the Pale, a vivid portrayer of the immigrant experience at the turn of the century. Further, she was a noted public speaker, a political campaigner, and a Zionist. Hers was a life at one time satisfyingly diverse that ended in sadness and obscurity.

As a career woman before feminism became vogue, Antin exploited the success that *The Promised Land* brought her. Placing her young daughter in boarding school and leaving her husband at home, she became politically active in the Progressive movement. In 1916 she supported the unsuccessful Progressive presidential candidate Charles Evans Hughes and, as a much sought and prolific public speaker, traveled around the country extolling the virtues of public education and the necessity of an open immigration policy interspersed with the necessity of support for Zionism. Although she was sensitive about her lack of domesticity, admitting as much in her letters, Antin always believed her primary work was her writing.

Perhaps Antin's teachers and benefactors could have predicted that she would rise to prominence from such inauspicious beginnings, but when the Antins settled in Chelsea, a working-class suburb of Boston, the growing family was oppressed with its struggle against poverty because her father, Israel Antin, failed in a series of small business ventures. In Russia, Israel Antin had been a businessman of moderate success, traveling to Moscow and environs and becoming acquainted with the secular world. As a young man he prided himself on his enlightenment and had separated himself from the rigid Orthodoxy of his family. He had hoped to provide an education for all his children. However, stringent Russian anti-Jewish laws and family illness plunged him into inextricable poverty and took its toll on him emotionally. This plight, compounded by the trauma of resettlement in the United States with the new language and customs, stood in the way of his "Americanization." Mary, though, was succeeding mightily in school, learning English quickly and winning the praise and support of her teachers. The Antins' move to a Boston slum with hopes of a better opportunity for financial success failed, and the family's desperation only increased as a succession of enterprises also languished. Fortunately, Mary was able to enter the academically prestigious Boston Latin School for Girls and to make wonderful use of the Boston Public Library that enthralled the eager student. Boston was also the site of various philanthropic and social agencies, such as the Hale House, which offered adult education and skills courses, and the Hebrew Immigration Aid Society (HIAS). HIAS provided similar opportunities, and through that organization philanthropists and social service–minded individuals interested themselves in poor but promising immigrants and offered financial assistance to the newcomers. Antin announced at the outset of her association with HIAS that she had no intention of becoming a seamstress or any other laborer. She would be a writer. In such surroundings Antin thrived.

Taking note of the precocious teenager, generous and pragmatic adults such as Philip Cowen fostered Antin's efforts and helped her publish *From Plotzk to Boston,* a collection of letters to an uncle, in journal form, about her journey from Russia to America.* Five years after her arrival in the United States, still a student at the Latin School for Girls in 1899, Antin was a published author. The proceeds from the book enabled her to remain in school instead of seeking other work that would contribute to the family's support.

At a Natural History Club outing sponsored by the Hale House, Antin met the paleontology lecturer Amadeus Grabau.† They fell in love and married in 1901.‡ Her marriage at nineteen to the thirty-one-year-old Grabau brought about a monumental change in Antin's life. Plucked out of the slums and away from a home life of pressing family cares, she found herself living in New York as a Columbia University faculty wife with all the trappings the position entailed, primarily, the immersion in a society of the intelligentsia. She enrolled in a literature course at Barnard College while studying German at home. As the years passed and she gained confidence in her own writing, Antin was encouraged by her husband and her new friends to write an autobiography, highlighting the immigrant experience. In 1911 the *Atlantic Monthly* published her short story "Malinke's Atonement" and featured a serialization of *The Promised Land*. The complete autobiography in a somewhat different version appeared in book form in 1912.

The highly popular book is the story of two worlds: the Russian world of Antin's childhood, a world that held precious little in positive memories save nostalgia for some cakes and aromas fondly remembered from her youth, and the New World of America where hope for a better life abounded. Russia was a place of deprivation, both material and intellectual, permeated by fear and oppression. The United States, despite worries about her father's ability to earn enough to support the family, was a place where the life of the mind for the young Antin was valued

*Philip Cowen (1853–1943), an American publisher and author, founded the Anglo-Jewish weekly the *American Hebrew* and remained the journal's editor and publisher for twenty-seven years, during which he was instrumental in the publication of works by Emma Lazarus, Mary Antin, and other Jewish writers.

†Amadeus Grabau (1870–1946) taught geology and paleontology at Columbia University from 1901 until his dismissal in 1918. He moved to China in 1920 where he served as professor of paleontology at the National Peking University and as chief paleontologist at the Geological Survey of China. He lived and worked in China until his death in 1946. A prodigious scholar, Grabau produced 146 papers and a series of major works, including six monographs on Paleozoic fossils and three books on the geological history of China.

‡Clara Antin relates that the fact that Grabau was a professor softened the blow of Mary's intermarriage. "But," she says, "my mother, I feel quite sure, had a good deal of anguish."

and the future, through educational opportunities, held promise without limit.

Quite aptly, Antin chose the genre of the spiritual autobiography for *The Promised Land*. English in origin, adapted by the Quakers and the Puritans, continued by the slaves in their narratives, and expanded to include various introspective works by poets and other nonfiction writers, the spiritual autobiography is a narrative of selected experiences. The narrative always has the element of a journey, often a sea voyage, which represents the arduous path, and then the hero experiences great change for the better. In many works of this genre, religious conversions or, at least, biblical metaphors are common as is, often, the hunger for education previously denied. Following in the footsteps of several famous American autobiographers—such as Phillis Wheatley, Benjamin Franklin, Booker T. Washington, and Frederick Douglass—Antin shaped *The Promised Land* to fulfill all these components.

The biblical title of the autobiography sets the stage for the chapter headings: "The Tree of Knowledge," "The Exodus," "Manna," and "The Burning Bush"; and the arduous voyage over land and sea describes the perils that befell the family as they made their way from Russia to Germany where they set sail for America. As the ocean divided the Old World from the New, it represented the separation from all she remembered as negative and what she left behind and all that lay before her in a promise to be fulfilled.

The hunger for and veneration of education as a common element in the spiritual autobiography is prominently featured in *The Promised Land*. Antin's father's handing her over to the first teacher is recorded as a sacred act. "[He] brought his children to school as if it were an act of consecration. . . . [He] regarded the teacher with reverence."* Teachers, school, learning, and the Boston Public Library all take center stage in the book and fulfill the adherence to the genre Antin employed in writing "a genuine personal memoir [in which] its chief interest lies in the fact that it is illustrative of scores of unwritten lives."† She used the form that earlier famous Americans had used and educated generations about the immigrant experience and Jewish history.

Antin's short story "Malinke's Atonement" in its few pages is a microcosm of many of Antin's ideals. It encompasses some of her attitudes about Judaism, her near idolization of education, and her admiration of

---

*Antin 1997, 162.
†Ibid., 2.

independent thinking. The story is of a young girl who tests the limits of Jewish law with regard to dietary prohibitions, and the actual and philosophical problems that ensue. Astonished when her transgression of falsifying the rabbi's injunction against eating the ritually tainted food fails to bring down the wrath of God in punishment, Malinke reasons that the punishment would likely fall on her family. She atones for the sin by throwing her favorite shoes into the river (shades of Slichot, the Jewish practice of symbolically casting one's sins into the water before the High Holy Days). When the rabbi learns of Malinke's sacrifice to enable the poor family to eat a proper meal, he is remorseful and rewards her by taking her on as his student, a privilege and duty normally assigned only to boys.

"Malinke's Atonement" portrays the Jewish religious leader as rational and compassionate; it rewards the innovative thinker, and it elevates education to a coveted prize. The story was the subject of scores of letters to her publisher while Antin was in the process of writing it. She fretted over how the American reading public would perceive Malinke without knowing the history of the Jewish people. She resolved the problem with a fuller treatment of Russian Jewish history in *The Promised Land*.

The great popularity of *The Promised Land* catapulted Antin to the status of a celebrity. Nevertheless, mindful of her recent past as part of a poor immigrant community, she became very interested in Progressivism's socially conscious ideas. She believed in the Progressive Party's tenet that government must give services to its people by, among other creative improvements, passing industrial workers' protection and social welfare legislation as well as utility regulation to control monopolies. Progressives also favored regulation of great interstate corporations and government conservation of natural resources. But perhaps the most important plank for Antin in the party's platform was its stand in favor of unrestricted immigration. It was this strongly held conviction that was the subject of Antin's next book, *They Who Knock at Our Gates: A Complete Gospel of Immigration*, published in 1914.

The premise of the book is an argument for a humane immigration policy based on the ideas of the country's Founding Fathers. Comparing the biblical Hebrews' entry into Canaan to the Pilgrims' landing in America, engendered by Old World religious intolerance, Antin expanded the analogy to the prospective immigrants' arrival in America, an emigration from Europe that sprang out of poverty and, for many, religious persecution. With those comparisons as a backdrop, she proposed that U.S. citizens should oppose the prevalent restrictionist sentiment in the country and support open immigration as a patriotic, even religious, duty. Although the book did not achieve the success of *The Promised Land,* it established Antin as a strong public supporter of open immigration, and led to her popularity as a speaker for the Progressive movement. She began as an admirer of Roosevelt, who lost the Republican Party's nomination in 1916, but she extended her loyalty to the winning candidate, Charles Evans Hughes, a former governor of New York and an associate justice of the Supreme Court. She threw herself into the campaign enthusiastically and, by 1916, was one of the Progressives' foremost spokesmen. Hughes lost the election to the Democrat, Woodrow Wilson, by a very narrow margin but went on to become secretary of state and from 1930 to 1941 served as a Supreme Court justice.

Antin's political activism, including work for a women's organization, excluded a concern for the woman suffrage movement that was gaining momentum and feminist support—a curious omission considering her independent spirit. As a woman who retained her maiden name in public and in her writings and who eschewed domesticity in favor of a career in writing and speaking, she, nevertheless, pointedly clarified her position to Theodore Roosevelt as being opposed to woman suffrage. Roosevelt's response, "I shall at once alter what I said which makes it look as though you are an advocate of suffrage," undoubtedly followed a stern correction by Antin. Another example of this paradox is in a letter of 1916 to Horace Kallen in which she defends her intellectual independence with fiery emphasis, berating Kallen for his reference to her as part of a "harem" of Roosevelt fans.* Her contemporary Emma Goldman, an anarchist and courageous speaker in favor of birth control for women, was also not a participant in woman suffrage advocacy. Perhaps these women decided to focus on their special interests in an era when so many public concerns needed to be addressed.

Complementing Antin's public life in politics and in promoting her books was her growing interest in Zionism. Modern Zionism began with Theodore Herzl, the Hungarian-born writer and journalist who, when covering the infamous 1894 Dreyfus treason trial in France with its overt anti-Semitism, was galvanized to act in behalf of a homeland for European

---

*Horace Meyer Kallen (1882–1974), a philosopher and educator, taught at Princeton and at the University of Wisconsin and was one of the founders in 1919 of the New School for Social Research. He coined the term *cultural pluralism,* by which he meant that each ethnic group in America had a special contribution to make to the country's variety and richness, allowing for the preservation of multiple cultures. He was active in the Jewish community and an ardent Zionist.

Jewry. Herzl organized the first World Zionist Congress held in Basel, Switzerland, in 1897. After years of great efforts on the part of Herzl and his associates, in 1917 the Zionist organization secured approval for its program of establishing a homeland in Palestine with the enactment of the Balfour Declaration by the British government.

Support for Zionism was slow to take hold in America until after 1912 when prominent American Jews such as Louis Brandeis began to promote the nationalist movement.* Antin joined the growing number of U.S. Jews who worked to garner American interest in Zionist work. She attended Zionist conferences, befriending and corresponding with Zionists while speaking and writing about the importance of a Jewish homeland.

It was a heady life: deeply involved in politics, associated with a national campaign organization, and admired as a Zionist supporter. But it was all to come to an end with the entry of the United States into World War I. The war brought about the pivotal experience in Antin's life. Amadeus Grabau, by then a noted paleontologist who had trained a large body of American and international students, many of them Chinese, publicized his pro-German sympathies. These attitudes were in great conflict with Antin's patriotic sentiments and public image. All over the United States there was virulent public antipathy to everything German: the language ceased to be taught in the schools, the Metropolitan Opera refused to stage Wagner operas, and German immigrants took care not to speak in their native tongue. The charged atmosphere was enormously stressful to the Grabaus, and soon a division of loyalties led to their separation and to Antin's resultant mental breakdown from, which, her letters imply, she never fully recovered.

Antin's fragile mental health kept her from the public-speaking career that had earlier provided a substantial income. Her enthusiasm for the work was gone, and new interests gradually developed. Hospitalizations, dependent living situations, and new acquaintances far removed from the public arena constituted Antin's changed life. In time her concerns turned away from politics and national agendas to spiritual issues related to mysticism, Christianity, and anthroposophy.

Antin's life cannot be said to have followed a logical continuum. It was a journey, but not in the usual sense where signposts lead the traveler from one destination to the next. Antin's journey was determined by events: some cataclysmic, such as the pogroms in Eastern Europe that forced the

*Louis Brandeis (1856–1941) was an American liberal lawyer, appointed to the United States Supreme Court in 1916, and a leader of the American Zionist movement.

Antins out of their native country, and World War I, which figured in the destruction of Antin's marriage. Earlier determinants in the journey were the good fortune of her native intelligence and her ambition, qualities that brought the adolescent Antin to the attention of philanthropists who promoted her and offered the prodigy glimpses into the intellectual and cultured life. To the great surprise of her supporters who were grooming her, however, it led not to a continuation of her studies and a timely marriage to an appropriate Jewish suitor, but to a sudden early marriage to a non-Jew who removed her from their sphere of influence. (Although she was nearly twenty, most of her friends and acquaintances knew her as a seventeen-year-old high school girl.)* The marriage lifted her out of an oppressive home life of poverty and, in time, provided the support for her to write the successful autobiography. But its later breakup became the catalyst for her decline into illness and obscurity.

Although the public did not follow Antin's life after 1920, her journey continued. An intense attachment to Will Gould, a Protestant minister and founder of the quasi–mental health facility Gould Farm, influenced her to explore Christianity. In the early 1930s, still troubled, she sought comfort as a follower of the mystic Meher Baba and lived in a group home with fellow Baba disciples. But after approximately three years she rejected the mystic's teachings, never referring to him in her letters again, and returned to Gould Farm. For the next ten years she was beset with illness as she moved from the farm to the homes of her sisters and back to the farm again. In her mid-sixties, Antin discovered the German philosopher Rudolph Steiner, whose out-of-body experiences intrigued the ailing and unhappy woman. She devoted herself to his work until her death in 1949.

Before turning to Antin's correspondence, which spans fifty years, I would like here to describe a collection of letters as a text about whose creation the author is unaware. The author writes to various correspondents on diverse subjects over a lifetime. The collector of the letters, however, reads, organizes, and interprets them as a unified entity, creating a new text. It is this new text that is at odds with some of the critical writing about Antin as the Russian Jewish immigrant who quickly assimilated into the dominant American culture and rose to fame through her popular autobiography. The 1912 work, which was one of the most popular books at the time of its publication, is still read as an example of a spiritual autobi-

---

*Antin's handwritten draft of *The Promised Land* recounts her father's successful plan to obtain two additional years of elementary education for the thirteen-year-old Antin. He did this by lying to the Chelsea, Massachusetts, school administrator, telling him that his daughter was eleven. Antin immortalized this episode in her short story "The Lie."

ography that depicts the immigrant experience. Much of the recent critical literature, written more than a half century after its publication and decades after Antin's two short pieces in the *Atlantic Monthly,* takes on an inappropriate dimension in that it exploits the tragic turn her life took, with its leanings toward mysticism and Christianity, to denigrate her early work.

Many critics believe that Antin betrayed her Jewish heritage, that she promoted assimilationism at the expense of Judaism. And because of her forays into other religions after her mental breakdown, they consider her a traitor to her people. These critics are no doubt unaware of Antin's Zionist work and her ardent promotion of open immigration that would have benefited European Jewry. Excerpting text from *The Promised Land,* critics have taken Antin to task for her adolescent reverence for George Washington, sentiments Antin describes as stronger than those for King David or God. One critic, buttressing her opinion that Antin was ready to discard her religion, uses the much quoted text, "I have thoroughly assimilated my past. . . . A long past vividly remembered is like a heavy garment that clings to your limbs when you would run." Summing up, she concludes that Antin's "religio-cultural striptease prevented her from becoming a profound writer of Jewish-American literature, or for that matter, any kind of literature."* Along the same line, another critic vents, "Mary Antin would transmute each little immigrant into a facsimile founding father by amputating the newcomer's past. . . . As for the Torah, Mary felt that it too would acquire greater sanctity if it were bound with the Declaration of Independence."†

The Promised Land, written by the twenty-nine-year-old Antin, closes when the subject of the autobiography is a high-school senior. Despite the subject's age, one critic describes Antin as suffering from an arrested sexuality, of being "ungendered" and "adolescent."‡ The appellations *lover* and *hero* in a letter describing her husband would argue against that conclusion, as would the recognition that, in 1912, the sexual longings of a high-school girl would be an anachronistic inclusion in an autobiography. It would also detract from the overall purpose of the work, as the book is, to a certain extent, a propaganda and "how-to" text in which the author attempts to show that Americanization for immigrants by way of public education is the road to success.

*Cohen 1977.
†Greenberg 1956.
‡Bergland 1991.

It is in part understandable why these critics may have come to their conclusions because they have not had access to a significant part of Antin's writing: her letters. I have unearthed some 150 letters that will, I believe, greatly modify the prevailing critical view of Antin and her work. The letters affirm her ardent patriotism but reveal her concerns that she give an accurate portrayal of Russian Jewish history. They document her firm belief in open immigration and the possibility of citizen action to bring about political change. They record her Zionist work. And, finally, they lay bare the depths of despair that the end of her marriage caused her.

Antin's legacy deserves a new interpretation so that, contrary to the efforts of her detractors, she will be restored to her rightful place among American historical figures, primarily as the first documenter of Russian Jewish history in English. She should also be acknowledged as an uncompromising proponent of open immigration when the position was unpopular, and as a Progressive when the party's success was in doubt. And, not to be minimized, she should be remembered as a Zionist who used every opportunity, in her talks around the country, to promote Zionism. We also need to empathize with the woman who, despite her outward strength and influential friends, was vulnerable to the same wounds of lost love as the woman next door.

Antin's life intersected with immigration, assimilation, and Zionism, some of the major themes in American history and American Jewish history. Her family was part of the great immigration at the turn of the century, and later, when the acclaimed autobiography thrust her into the limelight, she was again involved in immigration but this time, from 1912 to 1916, from a very different vantage point: as a married woman, successful author, celebrated speaker, and antirestrictionist. At that time, when restrictionist sentiment ran high, Antin regularly promoted open immigration as the best policy for enriching American culture, campaigning for presidential candidates Theodore Roosevelt and Charles Evans Hughes, whose views on the issue mirrored hers.

The major theme of assimilation was one from which Antin derived both great pleasure and strong criticism. For first-generation immigrants, assimilation into the dominant culture was rare. Such was the case with Antin's parents and older sister Fannie. Before Antin's marriage, her associations were mainly with Jews, albeit Jews who, if not totally assimilated, had at least integrated into an American lifestyle. Her mentors, the Lazaruses and Hechts, to name a few, were of Sephardic and German origins, respectively, and had been in the country for at least a generation.

This very positive and nurturing arrangement became precisely what her critics used to fault her.

Much maligned by some Jews for her views, compounded by her marriage to Amadeus Grabau, the Lutheran minister's son, Antin defended assimilation as a given right in a free society. She identified with Jews, used Yiddish phrases in her letters even to non-Jews, celebrated Jewish holidays in her home, and, during World War II, agonized about the fate of European Jewry. In 1941, after years of separation from Jewish life, she wrote, "I can no more return to the Jewish fold than I can return to my mother's womb; neither can I in decency continue to enjoy my accidental personal immunity from the penalties of being a Jew in a time of virulent anti-Semitism. The least I can do, in my need to share the suffering of my people, is to declare that I am as one of them."*

Antin addressed her Jewishness or Jewish concerns in many of her letters: from her preoccupation about religion in her early girlish letters to Israel Zangwill to her worries about presenting an accurate portrayal of Russian Jewry in the correspondence with her *Atlantic Monthly* editor, Ellery Sedgwick; and from her pride in Jewish women in a letter to Theodore Roosevelt to discussions of the Zionist writer Jessie Sampter's work with Horace Kallen.† Even when she lived far removed from her former life, in the Christian setting of Gould Farm, Antin expressed indignation at criticism relating to insufficient Jewish philanthropy for the farm.

Because of her strong Jewish background, Antin's public life intersected with the unifying theme for Jews: Zionism. She could naturally reach out from her assimilated milieu to take part in the great nationalist Jewish movement. For her there was no conflict in integrating American political talks with pleas for Zionist support.

Before turning to a brief overview of Antin's correspondence and the letters themselves, I would like to convey that, granting that the letters will surely bring her to life in all the many ways in which she lived, they can stand alone as a body of work that is a pleasure to read for its charm, forthright descriptions of an era, and intelligence of expression. The reader will soon realize, however, that the letters portray a life of disparate parts. The first part, beginning in her adolescence, is an expression of her

---

*Antin 1941.

†Israel Zangwill (1864–1926), English author of the play *The Melting Pot* and other works, became a Zionist after meeting Theodore Herzl and established a Zionist settlement in Galveston, Texas, before World War I.

literary aspirations, religious doubts, and concerns for her father's inability to succeed at life in the United States. They are interspersed with complaints about the social taboos imposed upon her as she reluctantly enters womanhood. A decade later, launched on a literary career, her letters portray a vibrant woman intent on presenting a sympathetic and accurate history of Russian Jewry. She was a secular person, politically active, with the goal of raising Americans' consciousness about the merits of open immigration. She was a woman of action, decisiveness, and moral courage.

The second part of Antin's life might be that of another woman's, so different is the persona that emerges from the letters following her mental breakdown and the dissolution of her marriage. This Mary Antin laments her inability to write in contrast to what she expected her lifework to be. She is entirely uninvolved with American politics, deeply spiritual, even religious, adopting some Christian and mystical ideas though retaining her Jewish identity.

In the end, it may be impossible to reconcile the early and later personae found in her letters. The public Mary Antin, while regarded in some circles as the ideal American, has been the object of criticism for her alleged assimilationism at the expense of Judaism. The later Antin, after 1920, not well known by the public, virtually reclusive at Gould Farm or with relatives, is a woman turned almost entirely inward, seeking spiritual solace for her sad life in mysticism and some aspects of Christianity. But no matter what conclusions we draw regarding the path Antin's life followed, the letters deepen and complicate our understanding of her work, validate her standing as an American political figure, and will restore her to an honored place in Jewish literature.

Manuscript Locations

AJA American Jewish Archives

AJH American Jewish Historical Society

BP Boston Public Library

BU Brown University

CZ Central Zionist Archives

CU Columbia University

GF Gould Farm

HH Henry Huntington Library

JT Jewish Theological Seminary

LC Library of Congress Manuscript Division

MH Massachusetts Historical Society

SS Sophia Smith Collection

WV West Virginia University Library

Selected Letters of Mary Antin

Mary Antin's parents, Esther and Israel Antin, in Dorchester, Massachusetts, with daughters Rosemary and Clara on the porch of the house that Mary Antin bought for them.

CHAPTER ONE

Adolescence and Marriage

1898–1906

Antin's intelligence and aptitude for the English language brought her to the attention of her teachers and to philanthropists and caseworkers at the Hebrew Immigrant Aid Society in Boston. Through these channels Israel Zangwill, the noted English writer, read Antin's collected letters to an uncle in Russia, which she had translated, with an eye to publication, from Yiddish to English. The journal appeared with Zangwill's introduction in 1899 as *From Plotzk to Boston*. (Antin decided to let stand the misspelling of Polotzk.) Zangwill encouraged Antin to write to him, offering her a vital source of literary inspiration. An important correspondence began that functioned as a sounding board for Antin's questioning faith in religion and admission of bewilderment over her emerging sexuality. Despair about her father's repeated business failures and the family's poverty is ever present in these pages. The Zangwill letters provide the reader with a picture of the privileged life that the adolescent Antin led despite her family's poverty. She enjoyed the protection and guidance of several wealthy, cultured Jewish families as well as the beneficence of some "proper Bostonians" such as Edward Everett Hale, whose library was at her disposal.* The Cowens, the Hechts, and Josephine Lazarus, to name a few, nurtured the young Antin.† Music lessons, concert attendance, access to private libraries, and summer vacations away from Boston are all duly reported to Zangwill.

*Edward Everett Hale (1822–1909) was an American author and Unitarian clergyman whose family included the orator Everett Edward and the martyr/spy Nathan Hale.

†The Hechts were prominent Boston Jewish philanthropists and social reformers. Josephine Lazarus (1846–1910), an essayist and sister of the poet Emma Lazarus, was the daughter of a cultured New York Sephardi family.

Coping with the disjunction of living with her family in the slums of Boston and associating almost daily with wealthy, cultured people must have taken its toll. Antin wrote to Zangwill that she was not able to attend school and had gone to the Cowens to convalesce. For a while, she contemplated accepting an offer from an elderly man whose mission it was to give promising girls from poor neighborhoods a better life by making them his wards, supporting their families, and taking them along on his world travels. In the summer of her junior year of high school, Antin accepted a position as private secretary to Amadeus Grabau, who was doing geological work in Maine.

A conflicted, maturing Mary Antin is evident in a letter of that period. Endeavoring to perpetuate her child-prodigy image as she reveled in the pampered treatment by her teachers and benefactors, Antin shunned her burgeoning sexuality. She protested vigorously to Hattie Hecht that she was still a young girl when admonished about the improper behavior of going out unchaperoned with Grabau. During this time, Antin was still preserving the lie that she was sixteen years old when in fact she was eighteen. However, within a year of her protests she was defending what Zangwill referred to as a "premature" marriage, declaring her early marriage acceptable when compared to her grandmother's at thirteen—an astonishing development in a negligible time span, from protesting adolescence to extolling marriage.

The high school girl's marriage to the geology professor Amadeus Grabau, eleven years her senior, and her move to New York prevented her from graduating from the Boston Latin School for Girls or from the Practical Arts high school to which their father transferred Antin and her sister Clara.* In New York she enrolled in some courses at Barnard College, but did not graduate. A year after her marriage, in 1902, Antin wrote to Zangwill that all her devoted wealthy friends and supporters had abandoned her, surmising the intermarriage to be the cause, even though, she wrote, "I have not changed my faith."†

Antin began to concentrate her efforts on getting her short pieces published. She befriended the publisher Louis Lipsky and through him met some New York Jewish writers, notably Bernard G. Richards.‡ Although

---

*Clara Antin, interview by Henry Laskowsky, Belmont, Vt., Oct. 1972, tape in my possession.

†Antin to Zangwill, Oct. 8, 1902.

‡Louis Lipsky (1876–1963), an American Zionist leader, journalist, and author, founded the *Maccabean* magazine, the first English-language Zionist periodical in the United States. He later edited the *American Hebrew*. Lipsky's magazines exercised a powerful influence on

it would be another ten years before she would succeed in getting any of her work published, Antin always took her writing very seriously, referring frequently in her letters to her "work." However, when Grabau and Lipsky urged her to introduce herself to prospective publishers as the author of *From Plotzk to Boston*, she refused to exploit what she perceived as "artificially puffed-up notoriety," considering the action "graft." She insisted that her work be judged on its own merit and steadfastly refused to waiver on this strongly held principle, even though doing so might be to her advantage.

1. To Israel Zangwill [CZ]

228 Dover Street
Boston, Mass.
December 30, 1898

My dear provisional friend:

You can scarcely imagine the degree of my surprise and pleasure when Mrs. Hecht told me this afternoon that I might write to you myself, in reply to your kind inquiries concerning me. I had not expected such a favor, and would never have been bold enough to ask it.

It is with a little penitent fear that I proceed to report my conduct since I received your little note of threat and promise. To be honest, I have broken your friendly admonitions in a few instances: I have stayed up a little too late a few times. But, dear Mr. Zangwill, if you consider how hard it is to break from habits a few years old, and what temptations there are in my case, you must give me some credit for trying as I do. If I am partly successful now, cannot you have a little patience with me, a little faith in my earnestness? I am so confident of your kindness that I do not fear any very severe judgement from you.

I know you will be glad to hear that I am well and happy. This is the first winter for a number of years that sees me in the enjoyment of such good health.

At school matters are about the same as usual; i.e., I find no difficulty in my studies—the work is just hard enough to make it thoroughly enjoyable. We are translating the first book of Caesar, and have just ended those glorious Persian Wars. The French and Algebra offer nothing especial as yet.

American Zionist actions. Bernard G. Richards (1877–1971), an American journalist and author, was widely active in Jewish affairs. In 1915 he helped found the American Jewish Congress and in 1932 founded the Jewish Information Bureau of Greater New York.

You reproached me for taking you "entirely on trust," because I had such a high opinion of you before I read your greater works. I am ready to take all the world on trust, if my good opinion of it previous to studying is as strongly confirmed afterwards as it has been in your case. For your dear *Children* [*Children of the Ghetto*]* have only shown me that I should respect and admire their father more than ever, if such a thing were possible. O Mr. Zangwill! You will never know with what delight I trod the streets of the Ghetto beside its inhabitants. A good many friends I met there—friends not only because you made me love them, but because I had known them in my old home, in Russia. I felt very much at home with them; and, having dropped all the manners and customs which they retain, I experienced much pleasure in reviewing them once more, often wondering how I could ever have kept them.

How could you make Hannah so cruel to poor David? It is all strange to me—that they who doubted so for a while should return to their old faith in the end. It is almost enough to make a poor little wavering thing like me seek assurance at the same source. Do you think I will some day, like Hannah and Esther and Levi? I wish that I knew; this doubt is so distracting.

Believing that I have not forfeited it because of mere partial failure, I hope for a renewal of your great promise, and remain, with sincere wishes for your success and happiness in the new year,

Your true little friend,

2. To Israel Zangwill [CZ]

228 Dover Street
Boston, Mass.
February 5, 1899

Dear Mr. Zangwill:

Now that I have seen your preface [to *From Plotzk to Boston*] I have to renew my thanks. I assure you it greatly surpasses anything I had imagined (and I thought of a great many things while writing). It was a complete and delightful surprise, and gave my friends and myself as much pleasure as everything else connected with this happy affair put together.

I cannot deny being proud of the kind words you said about me and

---

*Children of the Ghetto (1892) is an internationally successful novel that records the history of the Ansells, a veiled account of Zangwill's own family. An epic story, *Children* depicts the tragedy and comedy of Jewish life in London's Jewish ghetto.

the little book. But I am sure my friends need not fear that they may "spoil" me. Why, they must have exactly the opposite effect, because, as they show me that you have confidence in my common sense to carry me unharmed through whatever good-fortune may bring, I am all the more anxious to retain this opinion. And I know that I can do so only by being, as nearly as possible, the girl you and my other friends would have me.

I hear that you are really coming to Boston this month. I hope it is very soon, and that your visit will not be too short to permit of your half-promised talk with me.

I have dropped the question that so vexed me of late, but not altogether from a mental effort. There were so many other things to fill my mind that I naturally forgot that. Yet it is sure to return with all its puzzles whenever alluded to in my hearing.

Mrs. Hecht promised to be my teacher and help as far as possible. I know nobody whose pupil I would so willingly become. It is wonderful what friends one year's acquaintance has made us. Some people might think that the great difference between our respective walks of life would always keep us a certain distance apart. But the truth is that we could not be closer friends if she were as humble as I, or I as exalted as she. I could not give her a more boundless confidence in all matters than I do now, nor could I enjoy a friendship more sincere and earnest than I am blessed with at present. No words of mine could tell you how much it means to me.

I had a very pleasant experience this week. Miss Josephine Lazarus is here on a short visit, and she paid me the honor of a call. Unfortunately I was not at home, but yesterday I met her at her friend's house. Miss Lazarus is one of the most charming persons I ever met (and you know how charming some of my friends are). I earnestly hope to win her friendship, as she already has mine.

As she intends to write a criticism on my pamphlet she asked all about my writing, and suggested that I should begin to keep a journal. Now that the idea is brought before me, I think I would enjoy it very much. I believe you will not think this too much, if I write as little in addition as I have done since my promise to you. What is your verdict?

You will see, when you come, that I am enjoying very good health this winter. And I am sure my reports must agree with those of my friends.

With hopes of a very near meeting, I am

Your sincere friend,

3. To Israel Zangwill [CZ]　　　　　　　228 Dover Street
　　　　　　　　　　　　　　　　　　　　　　Boston, Mass.
　　　　　　　　　　　　　　　　　　　　　　February 24, 1899

Dear Mr. Zangwill:

It is almost two weeks since your second visit to unhappy, storm-swept Boston. (And Boston blizzards, by the way, I shall soon learn to pray for, if they continue to bring me as much joy as the last two have done). The time has been so full of various occupations and events that I thought it much longer. It seems impossible that so much could happen in less than two weeks.

I suppose this will make you wonder *what* has been happening to me. Why, when I think it over, there is nothing in the last few days of real importance—only one event I should say, of which I shall tell you presently. But somehow *everything* seems an event to me, and why, I do not understand. Miss Frankenstein ("Little Lina") accused me of a nervous disposition, excitability, or whatever she calls it. Perhaps that is the instrument which magnifies little everyday occurrences into *events,* although for my part I am not aware of any more nervousness in me than I usually show. (And have you noticed it in any unusual degree?) At any rate, my days seem very eventful, and I always have a rather pleasant sense of expectation that something is going to happen, though, as a matter of fact, the only thing I really am constantly hoping for, the only thing that could happen, is that my father should get some permanent employment. As it is, I can only rejoice in the knowledge that I have done something which is such a help at present—the only help, too. Of course, the use to which the money brought in by the book is thus put is not in accordance with some very excellent plans made by my friends; but, then,

> The best-laid schemes o' mice and men
> Gang aft a'gly.

Besides, even if I am not religious, I have a firm faith in I know not what that the future will take of itself. So many unexpected things have occurred to me already that I do not despair of something turning up when the time comes. Neither must you give me any credit for keeping alive this hopeful spirit. You know how many encouragements I have had, encouragements quite sufficient to overtop the trials of adversity.

There is only one thing wanting to my happiness just now. If I could only make my family share my hope! They all rejoice at my good fortune—my every little success is a source of the fondest pleasure; for *my* prospects they have not a doubt. But when it comes to the hope of *general* good-luck some day—alas, I am sadly alone.

Dear me! I have been forcing upon you confidence in matters perhaps too uninteresting even for the ear of friendship. I am afraid Miss Lina would regard this want of control over my thoughts as a sure proof of her "nervous" theory. Perhaps she would even increase the dose of cod-liver oil pills, which she has insisted on prescribing for me the last few months. (Mr. Z., Miss Frankenstein does not practice medicine on anybody save me.)

And now—I must tell you of the one real event of the last week or so. It is nothing less than my being introduced to Rev. Edward Everett Hale. It came about very unexpectedly—like my introduction to you, perhaps. As it is a story by itself I shall not stop to tell it now. But it has made me happier than ever. I have such an adoration for writers of note that I regard them as superior beings; and to know a "real, live author" makes me feel so much nearer heaven. (I shall be there very soon, if I keep on advancing two steps every four months, as I have begun.)

My reverend friend was very kind in our first brief interview. He even invited me to pay him a call, which, you may be sure, I shall do very soon.

It is long since we took any notice of this mirthful holiday, but today I was reminded that it is Purim.* Thinking over the happy times we had in Russia, in the observance of our beautiful holidays, makes me feel more than ever the folly of throwing aside such precious traditions, if nothing more, for such mistaken *ideas* of intellectual freedom as always take their place. I emphasize *ideas,* because that is all it amounts to. Four years have been enough to prove to me that we only become the slaves of all the prosaic wear-and-tear of the American "hurry-up" life, without any poetry, any rest, or calm, when we cast from us the beautiful holiday-observances. Independence Day is very well for an annual re-awakening of the deep patriotism we Americans bear for our country; Washington's Birthday does a great deal towards feeding our adoration of our illustrious "Father of his County"; and Christmas is of some good, as it gives many of us so much enjoyment, in our share of the universal joy of the season, even though it has no other meaning for us except as a time for merriment. But are either of these productive of any of that holy calm and soothing of the spirit

---

*Purim is the Jewish holiday that falls on the fourteenth day of the Hebrew month Adar, in February or March. It celebrates the deliverance of the Jewish community of Persia from the plot of Haman, prime minister of King Ahasuerus. The narrative is of the Book of Esther.

which comes with our own holidays? It is just as if a young lady who works hard all day should go to a ball in the evening, to rest her wearied limbs.

You see I look upon the holidays as something we owe ourselves, for our health and happiness. I have not come to regard them as I used to, not so soon.

Mrs. Hecht made my father promise that, to please her, he would keep the Passover. I almost wish she hadn't. It will have but little meaning to any of us; perhaps the children will look upon it as a jolly good thing, but nothing more. For my father's own views have not changed any, and they partake of them, as far as they understand at all. To me, such a ceremony will seem like a mockery. I have *some* feeling for these things which my family do not share, and the forms without that feeling are worse than nothing.

I am running into solemn thoughts again, although I did not intend to. So I must turn to something more indifferent.

I think the sales of my book are encouraging; but I am such a poor business woman that I shall not say too much of my own judgement, lest I lead you to believe what is not true. Those who do buy the book are quite pleased, and I have several kind letters singing its praises. One of these adds, "What a dear good man and wise, helpful friend Mr. Zangwill is to you! I am very, very glad you have won his . . . interest." This she says merely from reading your preface, I believe. What would she say if she knew *all* you are to me?

I have had many pleasant experiences in consequence of the publication. It is "so nice," as we girls say, to have people who really amount to anything say that you have done something worth doing. One gentleman certainly proved that he meant it. He is one Mr. Endicott, chairman of the school board of Chelsea (a small city near us) and one of the trustees of that city's Public Library. He is going to put my book in the Library, as he says he thinks people ought to read it. But do you know, I am not much flattered by this compliment. I rather think he means it to be a sort of model for the school children, because he is going to put an account of my career at school with the book. Perhaps, again, he thinks it generally interesting for Chelsea folks, because I first went to school there. When I came to Boston I was already next to the last class of the grammar school. So there is not much for my *literature,* after all.

But I appreciate the kindness, notwithstanding, especially as Mr. Endicott does not even know me, and so does it all of his own accord. I suppose you are just as busy as ever, and hardly know whether I may hope for a few lines from you. You will hear from me, at any rate, as often as I can write.

With many grateful remembrances, I am

Sincerely your friend,

4. To Israel Zangwill [CZ]   134 E. 104th Street
New York, N.Y.
August 22, 1899

Dear Mr. Zangwill:

You know how glad I was when you said I might call on you again, last Tuesday, and you ought to know that I meant to take advantage of your kindness at the earliest opportunity. I hoped at the time that it would come very soon; but as I have been trying to look about a little, and as there are so many things to see, Mr. Cowen, who, of course, lays down each day's programme, has not been able to arrange matters so that I could call on you again.

Now Mr. and Mrs. Cowen wish me to ask you to come over, with Mr. Loeb, Friday next for dinner, at half past six.* Or, if you find it absolutely impossible to come for dinner, come after. But do please come. (This from myself as well as from the Cowens.) You know I have wanted very much to meet Mr. Morris Rosenfeld.† Mr. Cowen (who, as you know, is always doing something to delight somebody) has written to a friend of Mr. Rosenfeld, asking him to come over Friday evening, bringing our poet with him. Now won't it be delightful if you all come? I really hope, believe you will, and am in the fifth heaven of joy from mere anticipation. I shall be in the seventh heaven if you accept this invitation, as I need hardly tell you.

My delightful visit will end Monday. I have had and am having many pleasant experiences. I want to tell you of one, a very important one when you come. You will be surprised, and, I hope, pleased.

With hopes for a favorable reply,

Yours sincerely,

5. To Israel Zangwill [CZ]   228 Dover Street
Boston, Mass.
September 11, 1899

Dear Mr. Zangwill:

On account of my late experiences in New York I appear so changed to myself, no doubt because I *know* there has been a change, that I think I

*Louis Loeb (1866–1909) was an American painter.

†Morris Rosenfeld (1862–1923) was a Yiddish poet known as the "Poet Laureate of Labor."

am a different person, leading a different life, from the one of five weeks ago.

What a piece of luck it was for me when the Cowens came across me! Perhaps you do not know that it was just the home life of the Cowens that really brought the happy solutions to my many troublesome questions. I could not but see to what all that beautiful harmony and love were due; and so I finally turned to the same source for my lost peace of mind and contentment of spirit.

And they are now mine, so absolutely that they have already begun to exert considerable influence over the rest of the household. Would you have believed it so soon? It seems to make a great difference in all our lives, and I have no doubt it will lead to some great result in the end. I am so happy to think of this, because, Mr. Zangwill, there is room for change in our household, not only with regard to religion, but in several other ways. There is *need* for it, and there is needed someone to bring that change. On account of my numerous advantages I am better qualified to be that one than any other member of my family. I therefore feel that my position is a very useful, responsible one; but with my new spirit of faith a new hope comes also, and I do not despair of seeing my dearest friends much happier in the near future than they are now.

This new happiness I hope to make them create for themselves is a spiritual one, of course. I wish that it were also time for me to provide for their material happiness. I am usually the most cheerful of all the household; but this is one of the times when I get so discouraged at my father's failing in business of any kind that I begin to think our case a very hopeless one indeed. You may remember that I prophesied Papa's speedy dismissal from his position as watchman the night you and Mr. Loeb were at the Cowens'. The very next morning my prophecy proved to be fulfilled, by a letter from home. My father is still out of work. Mr. Cowen and some of my other friends think Papa ought to learn a trade, but he thinks he is too old, being almost forty. He is certainly not a strong man, and this fact has been his chief obstacle in life. Still, I cannot but wish he *would* try to learn some trade, because there is certainly enough possibility of his succeeding in one of the less difficult trades to warrant the risk of the time and labor that he would lose in case of failing.

Papa proposes now to take up peddling—there is a new kind of gas-lamp shade that he wants to try. But I have no faith in the project; he has tried similar things before with no success. The fact is that things look so hopeless to me now that I am beginning to think seriously whether *I* ought not to go to work at something that pays *now*, not at my books that will pay in the future. We can't live on that. I don't quite see what I can do, I know so few practical things. But if I should make up my mind that it was my duty to do something I would probably think of something. I suppose I would have to give up school for a while, but I would go on with my studies by myself. The only thing that holds me back is the thought that all the labor and influence some of my friends have used in my behalf would be misused, if not entirely lost, in case of my leaving school now. You yourself and the Hechts and the Cowens and others did not take so much trouble on my account just to see my chance of ever re-paying it turned away; and I feel that I must keep on in the course you have laid down for me if I am to arrive at the goal you have in view for me.

It is a very hard case indeed. I scarcely know what I am to do.

But I ought not to bother you with these things, I am afraid. It seems all right when I speak to you, because you seem to take it so naturally; but when I write I begin to think that while you have undertaken to be my ad-viser, you did not mean to look after the whole family into the bargain. So I will not trouble you *that* way any more if I can help it.

I want your advice on a new matter. I made such a grievous mistake about my journal because you did not know just what I did with it, that I don't want to risk anything else without asking you about it, even if I think it all right. There is an excellent institution up here in the South End called Hale House Republic, which does some very good work among the children and poor people of its neighborhood, and has the hearty support of many prominent people, like the famous Dr. E. E. Hale (for whose son it is named) and others. Once a month they publish the "Hale House Log," telling of the different work of the clubs, classes, meetings, etc., of its many members. As I am very much interested in Hale House work, and have been connected with some parts of it, they want me occasionally to write up one of the items for the "Log." It is a very harmless publica-tion of half a dozen pages or so, and is sent to Hale House friends. Con-tributors do not sign their names, so there really is no publicity about it. I wish I had a copy of the "Log" to send you. I think it is all right for me to write for the "Log" a short account of the Maine trip of the Hale House Nat. Hist. Club, of which I told you; or of a small party of children whom I took to the country for a day, on the invitation of a friend of Hale House; or of the annual celebration of a Hale House boys' club, where I took some part; and of other such like matters.

If you do not think it right of course I shall discontinue it; but I can't help it if a friend of mine published one of my letters to her in the report of the Lend-a-Hand Society, without asking me about it. She did not give my name, though. Shall I ask her not to do it again?

Perhaps I can send you one of the things I have written for the "Log" in a few days. But I think you understand well enough now.

With best wishes for the young year, and warmest hopes for the success of your dramatic venture, I remain

Your sincere friend,

P.S. I send this through Mr. Cowen because I do not know what your address is now. If you are still with Mr. Loeb, please give him my warmest regards.

6. To Israel Zangwill [CZ]

228 Dover Street
Boston, Mass.
September 17, 1899

Dear Mr. Zangwill:

Again you are so kind, so good to me that I have no words left in which to thank you with all the appreciation that I feel. It does often seem as though no amount of study can give one a command of language sufficient for all occasions. And you have made me feel this way more than anybody else I know.

I am sorry I wrote in such a hopeless tone about our affairs, as "things 'ave took a turn" again, and so I might have spared you all that. And yet I wouldn't have missed for a great deal the sympathy it called out in you, particularly your expression of it.

Papa has started off on a new line—a laundry agency. It cannot yet be seen what his success may be, but we know that others have found it a good business. I know also that your wishes for Papa's success are his, and wonder if *you* know what a cheering thought that is.

Whether we could avail ourselves of your efforts to help us in a new way or not (for in one way you have done much for us already) we are just as grateful—a man of great affairs like yours to give us so much thought! You have such a way of turning off the mildest outburst of sentiment, with a funny word or two, that I dare not tell you half the things my folks said about you: I never can make up my mind whether you really dislike sentiment, or whether your way of receiving its expression is just one of your own peculiarities. And you have so many, haven't you?

Instead of leaving school, I have entered on another year, with the addition of Greek and English to last year's Latin, French, Algebra, and history. I see I am to have a very busy year, and Greek will probably answer to your description of it—"a terrible language to learn," you called it once. But we have a most interesting course all together, as you can readily see by my list of studies. If the present state of my health continues, I hope to make a good year of it.

I was so perfectly contented with everything till your letter came. Now I have a new wish: I wish it were October! I saw Mr. Herne in *Shore Acres* last year, and was very much in love with him as Nathaniel Berry.* What an experience it will be to know him as James A. Herne! and as your friend, besides! I am so full of curiosity and pleasant anticipation that I cannot check my impatience, a wise thing though I know it would be. How shall I ever thank you for the new great experience you have put in my way? It may be a fault, but I am positively wild about people who make books and do other such big things. I feel as if I had just read a new chapter in the book of my life, every time I meet one of them. I wish it were time to turn to the page headed "James A. Herne." My journal—my truly confidential friend now, Mr. Zangwill—is waiting to receive my impressions of it. And, of course, you shall also know them.

Half of September is over, that's my consolation. If the rest goes as speedily as the first part did, happy October will be here before I have quite realized that it is time to present your letter.

Oh, are you sure your actor-friend will want to see me? I shall try to find out when the time comes, anyway.

Mr. Zangwill, if you knew how many people are asking whether *Children of the Ghetto* is coming here, you would come and answer them, I think. Why, what has poor Boston done to you to be so neglected? You don't treat "the Athens of America," "the Hub of the Solar System," at all as it [is] expected to be treated. Poor Boston! I say, poor, misused Boston!

Mrs. Hecht is one of those who ask, "Isn't it coming here at all?" And she wishes to be remembered to you with the kindest wishes for the success of your *Children*.

You were so good to write to me while you are so very busy—so kind to remember me—that I must thank you just once more before I close, only once more I thank you, for the present.

I suppose I can get at your address somehow as you travel about, so I shall write to you whenever I can. It is one of my great pleasures.

*James Herne (1839–1901) was an American actor and playwright.

Heartily wishing your play all the success which Mr. Cowen and many others predicted for it, I am

Your little school girl still,

7. To Israel Zangwill [CZ]

228 Dover Street
Boston, Mass.
October 2, 1899

Dear Mr. Zangwill:

Thank you for that little postscript in Mr. Loeb's kind letter. I was pleased with it and surprised, coming in this way. Don't you think Mr. Loeb was very good to write to me? He is a character, anyway, and I think a great deal of him. Miss Unger and I are very much in love with him. Perhaps you know that we called on Mr. Loeb the day after you spent the evening with us, at the Cowens'; and he was kind and charming personally, and showed us so many beautiful things from his hand, that we went away enraptured. Seriously, Mr. Zangwill, I would not have missed knowing dear Mr. Loeb for all the fun I had in New York!

You bid me be happy. It is easy to obey. I am happy almost always now. Once I used to dread the advent of the chill, dreary autumn, with all a semi-invalid's presentiments of discomfort and even illness. Now I am so well that I actually rejoice at the prospect of storms (perhaps *blizzards*) to brave, and fierce gales to make your heart sing with the sense of power you experience when walking briskly in their teeth. There is a love for struggle, for conquest somewhere within me, and I like to indulge it in this harmless manner. Today was very cold, almost like winter, and I was so pleased to feel my face and hands pricked by the early frost that I didn't even think of my lessons on my way to and from school, but gave my whole mind up to the enjoyment of the walk. It seemed good just to be alive, especially when I thought of the gorgeous autumn woods that I am promising myself to get a look at very soon, when I can get off for a day.

Sometimes such a little thing will make me happy that there seems no need to worry about greater, less bright things. So at present I would be happy with my health and my work and the weather even if everything else were going wrong. But "everything else," business principally, seems to be on the point of taking a happy turn. It looks very like success along the line of Papa's new business. Dear Mrs. Hecht, with her never-ending patience and goodness, will probably establish Papa in it permanently. To judge from the beginning another failure seems impossible. You know I have many friends—*we* have many friends—and that will of course aid largely. Altogether, nothing but a special intervention of the god of mischief can upset the business this time. Meanwhile we will call that impossible, and enjoy our altered prospects.

My school work gives me much genuine pleasure, as last year. Why, Greek is not so very terrible. I take great pleasure in discovering the source of words that have long been familiar to me—I like to know the why and wherefrom of things. I remember as a child how I would spend hours in tracing a word to its origin, though only from a Hebrew-ized Russian word to its correct form. Illiterate Jews often corrupted Russian words and expressions into a form more in accordance with their own vernacular, till to trace it back to its correct form, without any knowledge of books, but with mere comparing, arranging and pulling asunder of parts, and such like mental processes, became a very arduous task for a little girl. I used to speak a good Russian and this early taste for languages even then kept my mind, free from any work imposed on it, busy in the way I have mentioned. I remember distinctly my extreme joy on discovering the source of certain puzzling words. So now, when I can pursue this old amusement daily with one of my studies, that study is not likely to be a burden on me.

Latin is more fascinating than ever, as we get better and better acquainted with old Virgil. French, under a teacher far superior to last year's, is beginning to win its lawful place in my heart, but grudgingly granted it formerly. Roman history and algebra are favorites, and, best of all, *English* comes in at last. I have long thirsted for composition-writing and class reading and debate. We are studying the *Spectator* now, and we'll have Goldsmith and Scott and I don't know what other good things before the year is out. It is a splendid course all around.

A friend of mine, Rita Scherman—one of the loveliest girls I ever met, and my *only girl friend*—has probably written to you to solicit a contribution for a paper some young Philadelphians are about to issue. Rita said she would use my name in connection with her request, I do not know how. She had as good as promised her co-workers to procure something from me, never doubting that I would send it. However, I am so busy that I had to decline the honor of being enrolled as a contributor; and now Rita writes in the most unforgiving terms, and it wounds me sorely to think of her disappointment in me. She is such a bright, sweet, witching little thing (just my age) that it cost me a pang to refuse her first request. With regard to asking you for a contribution I did not say anything to Rita, as I did not know whether you would care to be bothered with the enthusiastic enterprises of a lot of boys and girls. To tell the truth, I know little about the scheme. Rita only told me that there was to be a Judean or a Something and she expected me to write for it. But there must be something earnest at the bottom of it, because Rita is all fire about it. So I cannot but wish that the dear girl had better success with you, late as the wish comes. I am waiting anxiously for the first number to see if you have written for it. Rita is an ardent admirer of yours, and could never have enough of hearing me tell about you. She was with the Cowens part of the time I was there, and I formed my first friendship with a *young* person. She is a very exceptional girl; you would have liked her too.

Yes, indeed, I knew of your success, and I was intending to write a word of congratulation. So many of my friends had predicted it that I was not surprised to see the press pronounce in praise of *Children of the Ghetto;* but I had been so anxious to see the prophecy fulfilled that—will you believe it?—I could not refrain from a little prayer of thanksgiving on seeing the first favorable criticism! It must sound strange, to hear me talk of *praying.* But you make me happy so often that I love to follow your doings closely, and every good stroke you make causes me as much joy as if it were my work and my success, truly. I triumph over those who spoke skeptically of your play before it appeared! I am so glad, and I congratulate you.

Thank you for that clipping. It seems strange to find myself on the other side of the ocean, but pleasant, too. "A.M." 's criticism is very sensible, if flattering now and then. He (or she) misunderstands me on one point, however: that "natural disdain of last year's work." The history of how the thing came to be written, and why I kept it unaltered in translating, would prove (or misprove) this mistake the critic makes. However, it is not worthwhile discussing here such an old tale. You were very good to send the cutting, though; it particularly gives me pleasure to see that you still trust me not to let such flattering notice spoil me. Why, it only makes me guard against it the more jealously when I see your confidence. I thank you for it sincerely.

Now October is here, and you shall hear from me soon about Mr. Herne.

With hopes for the continuation of your success, and best wishes for your general welfare, I am

Yours ever,

8. To Israel Zangwill [CZ]

228 Dover Street
Boston, Mass.
[undated]

My dear friend:

I hope you have not thought me unappreciative because I have been so long acknowledging the kindness now bestowed on me by such a letter. I know you will not, if I tell you that it was in order to keep your admonitions that I put off writing till I really had time.

To tell you the truth, I did not even hope that you would write to me directly. I thought myself highly favored if you remembered me in Mrs. Hecht's letter. Then how do you suppose I felt when I read your beautiful letter to *me*? Why, something as I did on the twenty-fifth of last November. As *you* have no reason to remember that day particularly, I must tell you that it was the day I met you for the first time.

Let me thank you for your ready pardon of my offences. It has strengthened my good resolutions more than anything else could have done because it has so well reassured me that your wonderful promise of friendship was not a mere happy dream as the fact that it all was so marvellous sometimes made me think. Believe me that not an opportunity will I miss to do that which would make me more deserving of all your goodness.

Mr. Cowen told me what a great kindness you are about to add to those I have already enjoyed. Dear Mr. Zangwill, you know what a poor, weak little writer I am. I wish you would also know that this is the reason for which you will never have any idea of the depth of my gratitude for all I owe you and my keen appreciation of the great honor you intend to confer upon me. Truly, there never was a more fortunate girl anywhere, one as loaded with blessings as I am. If all the virtues that man is capable of possessing were mine, and all the faults that ever deserved punishment were strangers to me, perhaps then I might feel that all my happiness was the generous reward due to me. But as it is, I can only strive and hope to be worthy of at least a part of it.

Of course I showed my friends your letter. Mrs. Hecht bids me say, in answer to your post-script, that she believes I do appreciate all she has done for me. The young ladies coincide with her opinion.

Last Sunday was the first anniversary of my meeting them, and, you may be sure, I remembered the day. I went to the Hechts and asked them to congratulate me, and when I told them why, they all declared that they congratulated themselves. Of course this was their kind way of looking at the matter, but I took it to have enough seriousness to mean that they think I *try* to deserve my good fortune.

I do not tell you this in boast. I am only happy to show you some little proofs of my efforts.

If I should write to you whenever anything troubles me, I should have to write so often that you would regret having given me permission. I do not know how it happened, but I have been made to think so much about religion lately that I am very much troubled. Why do you tell me not to bother about "solving the problems of the universe"? They are problems whose issue, if arrived at, would bring peace to my mind; otherwise it remained in a state of turbulence. I have not enough command over myself to be able to put unwelcome thoughts aside.

Perhaps you remember from our talk what a skeptic I am. But my skepticism is not the offspring of my convictions, by any means. It is born of the influence which certain minds have made over mine. At heart I am dissatisfied with it, but I cannot see the way out of it clearly.

Perhaps I will have a little light in my difficulty soon. I am going to take up some course of religious study with some friend, hoping that, as I am so anxious to come to some conclusion, it will exert the right influence.

I do wonder what it will make of me.

Have you not any suggestions to make? Surely you can help me a little in this matter. In my need I even dare to make bold enough to ask for aid as if it were my due.

My father wishes me to thank you in his name for remembering him, and for being so good to me.

With many thanks for many favors, I am

Your true friend,

9. To Israel Zangwill [CZ]

228 Dover Street
Boston, Mass.
January 21, 1900

Dear Mr. Zangwill:

I never was afraid of you, never, even the first time I saw you I wasn't afraid of the great Israel Zangwill. I was awed, but not afraid. Now I am decidedly afraid.

You know what I am driving at—about my not writing to you so long. And I am afraid you were so displeased that you wouldn't read this letter at all. However, as I may be exaggerating your displeasure, I'll make believe you *are* reading my prayer for forgiveness, and "tell you all about it."

There is so much to tell, yet so little that will exculpate your guilty little friend. I feel very guilty. It is about four months since I wrote you last—four months! And you were so kind when I gave you the opportunity. No matter how busy you were, you used to answer almost every one of my letters. I was telling one of my friends the other day as a sort of excuse for not writing or coming to see her since last June (she lives forty-five minutes' ride from us) that I hadn't written to *you* since September. "It is very wicked of you, Mary," she said solemnly. And her words are never trifling.

It is very wicked, I know. I am so full of the sense of my guilt that I cannot take my mind off it, to tell you the many things I wanted to tell. I wish I could persuade myself that I have written to you, and that my letter went astray. The last few months my letters were either lost, returned to me marked "Uncalled for," or delivered a week or so after they were due. I lost a story that I wrote for "Helpful Thoughts," in the same stream of mishaps by mail. (I had sent it in such a hurry that I didn't have time to make a copy even.) I have begun to think that there's a special divinity of evil, appointed by the lord of Olympus to misdirect everything I entrust to the mails. But I am wandering from the point. I was going to say that I cannot persuade myself that I did write to you lately. I know I did not, just as I know how ungrateful you must naturally think me.

I wish I were either good or bad, so that I knew it was *something* decided. But I'm neither good nor bad. I know I am not good, but I do not know that I am bad. Half the time I do something which makes me spend the other half in repentance and regrets and excusing myself. Isn't it dreadful so? You must have found it out of me. How every other letter I write you (when I do write) is a plea for merciful forgiveness for my latest misdeed.

Thunder turtles!! Do you mind if I say that? I were dumb, in my present overflow of impatient self-accusation, if it were forbidden me to make use of my pet escaping-valve. Perhaps it's very unladylike, but I haven't outgrown my boyhood yet. Besides, you'll never tell, I know.

Where are you, in Italy? I wish you were right here in Boston. Not, however, because I am beginning to long for a genuine blizzard, after our months of summerlike winter. That's another story. But if you were here I shouldn't have to write this impossible letter. For it is impossible. You see this is page 7, and I haven't told you anything yet.

I'll tell you what, I'll go out for a walk now. It's a beautiful afternoon, pleasant as the springtime, and the sunshine will clear away my cobwebs.

Sunday evening. —I'm all right now, Mr. Zangwill. I walked on the old

Cambridge bridge, where Longfellow "stood . . . at midnight." It is one of my favorite walks, both for association and attractiveness. This afternoon the wind blew sharp from the river, and the sunshine lay bright and laughing on the water. It put me into such a gay mood that I have been an hour playing with the babies, just for the sake of laughing. Now I feel ready for anything, this impossible letter even.

You couldn't possibly stand it all at once, if I were to tell you of all that has happened to me during this period of silence between us. I have been very busy all the time. (This is not an excuse. Nothing can excuse me, only you yourself.) I have enjoyed my work heartily, but it makes me nervous, as we say it, to be always in a hurry. "Bottled lightning" *is* a bad thing in a girl—or in anyone. However, I am feeling very well this winter, so my work cannot be any too much for me. I spent the Christmas vacation with the Cowens, and had a delightful time, as you can imagine. I'll tell you the most beautiful event of my visit, next to just being in the Cowen atmosphere: I heard Paderewski! If there were nothing else in the world to live for, I should consent to put up with life just to hear Paderewski.

I am taking lessons with my former teacher's teacher now, Felix Fox. You should hear him play! Not quite like Paderewski, but it's beautiful.

My progress in music is very slow, though. Sometimes I think I am not getting on at all, but Mr. Fox is very patient and encouraging. It's very hard for me because I have no piano, and so cannot practise enough. Pianos cost so much.

I am just going to tell you about the Hernes, and leave the rest for next time. Mr. Cowen said I mustn't write such long letters as I sometimes do, because I am really too busy. I wrote him forty-eight pages once, he says, in one letter. I was in great trouble at the time. I must not stop to tell you about it now, it's such a long story. In a few words, Mrs. Hecht said I was getting too big to be a girl, I must be a young lady. I mustn't go out alone with Mr. Grabau. (You remember him? He is my dear friend the scientist, who introduced me to the delights of nature study, the chief happiness in my life now.) I must be properly chaperoned on all occasions. I must and I mustn't a hundred horrid things. Are you going to be one of those who think that a girl *must* be a lady when she gets to be sixteen and a half, whether she is anxious for the honor or shudders at the thought of it? Then you will laugh at me when I tell you that it nearly broke my heart to become "grown up," and it made me positively ill, so that I couldn't go to school for a few days. It worries me still. Wouldn't *you* let me be a girl till I was tired of it?

But I must beware of the forty-eight-page mark.

I can never, never thank you enough for introducing me to Mr. Herne. He was very kind to me and he is such a great man! His simplicity of manner reminds me of you, as does his pleasant way of being good to little people. Then what an artist he is! *Sag Harbor* is a masterpiece, truly, and Mr. Herne is grand in it. So is Miss Julie. I was delighted with her "Martha." Miss Chrystal was a beautiful "Jane," but I was rather puzzled with her character. I don't see how she could be in love the way she was and yet be so like a child. But as Mr. Herne made her that way, it must be right, only I haven't seen a "Jane" in my life yet.

Mr. Herne was very kind to send me tickets, but it was a greater kindness to let me come and see him and the young ladies, in their own characters. I fell very much in love with them. Isn't Miss Julie sweet? Such a lovely woman as "Martha" is Julie Herne is lovelier. And I like Chrystal Herne far better than "Jane." She has such earnest ambitions, and big hopes, and is so *real* to me. Altogether they are two beautiful girls to know, and their father—he is something of a god. Still, I was delighted to find how human "actor people" are.

Sag Harbor is a grand success. It just left us yesterday after over a hundred performances, leaving an undying impression behind it.

I am so grateful for my experiences with the Hernes that I must say a thousand times thank you, to you. And a thousand times more ungrateful I will appear to you, for not writing to tell you this before.

My father is succeeding pretty well in a laundry agency. I cannot help being glad that he was out of work when I saw you in New York. Perhaps I should not have known Mr. Herne but for your desire to help us.

It will be so long before you get this. I have to send it to your English address, although Miss Herne told me you were in Italy. And it is so very long before an answer can reach me—

If you ever send one! Well, I won't try to count up the probabilities and the improbabilities. You have always been very lenient and forgiving with me, but since my friend said "It is very wicked of you, Mary," I've been positively afraid to think of what you will think of me when I remind you so tardily of my existence.

I shall not make any promises of being good in the future. My intentions cannot be better than they have been so far. When something always comes up to make them powerless—it's hard enough on me, anyway.

There are two girls in my class who are going to interrupt their school work for a year, to go abroad. Now I have a good mind to join them, for they will spend some time in Italy, and will probably get there sooner than an answer to this volume can reach me.

We can travel so fast these days, and send such rapid messages. Yet it will be an eternity before I can know whether you forgive me, and still consider yourself my guardian-friend, as of old.

It's so long ago since you called me a little school girl. Now, remember, I am a young lady. It's perfectly dreadful! I do believe my sudden growing up is to blame for my long silence. I was so busy learning youngladyisms. But Mrs. Hecht said I mustn't rebel, and you have had enough for once from
Your friend as ever,

10. To Israel Zangwill [CZ]

228 Dover Street
Boston, Mass.
April 3, 1900

Dear Mr. Zangwill:

Does a genius interest you? A real, live genius has just called on us, and I am so full of enthusiastic admiration that it has put out of my mind the thousand little things I was going to write you before he came. Perhaps you will be glad to hear something out of the ordinary from me.

He is a Jew and an artist and a husband and a father. All these distinctions given, you readily come to the inevitable conclusion that—yes, you have it: his usual occupation is starving. He was educated as an artist in Russia, I don't know just where, but not in St. Petersburg. Therefore, after gaining fame and fortune as the only portrait painter in Riga, his admiring friends, the officials of the city, bethinking themselves that a Jew could not practise his art unless he had studied in St. Petersburg (where a Jew is not allowed to study), he was forbidden the city as long as he continued his work; and he went to seek his fortunes elsewhere. Various were his experiences, many of them hinging on the accident of his origin, of course. He lived in Vienna a great many years, and knew many promising, persecuted young artists like himself. He drifted about and struggled and attained and lost, till five years ago he landed in America. Fortune had forgotten to come and welcome the young man who was taking such pains to find out her haunt; and the old lady must have been very busy these last five years, for she hasn't dropped in on him yet.

Mr. Keene (once Cohen) has tried and tried to make his art (portraits is his specialty) feed and clothe and house his little family of four, but neither bread nor clothing nor house will come from his brush. If I had not been one of my father's children, I would be at a loss to imaging how he "manages" on occasional five-dollar bills. This is what he has now. And it is disheartening, pathetic to hear him say, "I can do nothing now. My ideals and aspirations are mere words, when I have a wife and two children to feed." Such a man!

Mr. Keene is about thirty-five, medium height, blonde and pale, with a French beard, large, protruding blue eyes, with an occasional gray shadow in them, and a forehead!—such a forehead!—large and smooth and sloping, a premature indication of baldness adding something to the look it has of being the index to a thinking mind.

A true index. My new genius is highly intellectual. If I tell you that he is acquainted with Latin and German and Persian and French and English and, of course, Russian; that he has very original ideas on the development of literature, on social problems, and on systems of education; that (as far as I can judge) he has all the theories of art at his fingers' ends—if I mention these, with a few other accomplishments, you must admit that he is a man of brains. But I have still something to add: he discovered my father in an error concerning a quotation from Hillel. And my father is a Hebrew scholar of no mean grade.

Mr. Keene is fascinating in conversation. He can call up an illustration for everything he wishes to impress on his hearers. He argues strikingly, he convinces almost always. His choice of words is that of a man who mixes in intellectual society; which he must find only in books at present, for Mr. Keene has no friends here to speak of. His manners are attractive, his gestures graceful and expressive. The genius shines in every sentence he speaks.

To my mind, there is one flaw in this brilliant jewel. He is a little too pessimistic for me. I told him so. He smiled—that knowing smile of the experienced, such as I always see on my father's face when we are arguing—and said it was natural for me to think so *now*. I would learn later and then *I* smiled. I have my strong opinions, too.

As soon as I get acquainted with Mrs. Keene I shall try to decide (for myself merely) whether Mr. Keene hasn't another flaw. Unless his wife is one of those exceptional angels in human form that we read about, whose companionship is an inspiration in difficulties and a solace in distress—unless she is such, Mr. Keene was rash and commonplace to burden the wings of his genius with family troubles. What could he not have done if he had only himself to shift for? What can he ever do now?

I wish I were a rich woman, with more heads than Hecate. Mr. Keene should then do my portraits, and have a chance to be introduced into the world. How blind it is, the world!

I have felt a strange feeling of unworthiness—let me hope that it is a generous feeling—since knowing this new friend. Why, I cried to myself, should such a gifted man be allowed to struggle on unrecognized and unaided, when *my* poor little efforts are fostered and guided and tended? I have not deserved it, if Mr. Keene has not. If I have, he has merited tenfold. And if I am encouraged and he neglected, the world is unjust.

Have you ever wanted to share a blessing with a friend and been unable to satisfy your generous impulse? Is it not as distracting a sensation as longing after the blessing itself when it seemed out of reach? I have experienced this very feeling, many a time before, but never so strongly as since my acquaintance with Mr. Keene. If I could only give him some of the love and the care and the help and the encouragement that my friends lavish on me! If I could transfer to his soul some of the warmth of hope and trust that they fill me with! If I could make my friends his friends!— and he deserves it all so much better than ever I can.

Lest I make you think that you are witnessing a deification, I shall say no more about my new hero with the one fault. I only hope you are interested in him. I should be disappointed if I could not make you see what a great man he is, and what an abused man.

I fear you will have to tell me again that my letters are long with little in them. Have I improved at all? In the matter of postage stamps you may see improvement,

Ever your friend,

Please excuse my paper. I have been writing for three whole days, as it is vacation week, so my stationery has failed me. And I am so busy writing that I cannot go downtown.

11. To Israel Zangwill [CZ]

228 Dover Street
Boston, Mass.
May 2, 1900

Dear Mr. Zangwill:

It makes me happy to find that I belong to your "real world" which you favor with an occasional thought even when you are busiest. I long to give you of my best thoughts in return, out of my calmer, less eventful life.

Indeed I realize that you know what a painter's life is—I am sure that my friend will be very much pleased with your sympathy, and he may wish the Atlantic dried up. Perhaps we can do something with [illegible] "cheap portraits" scheme, too. I am anxious to see him and give him your message. Meanwhile I thank you for taking such an interest in my friends.

I have been to see Cora Wilburn lately in her retirement—*exile,* I ought to say—forty-five miles from Boston in Millbrook, Plymouth County,

Massachusetts. She is the most interesting woman I know, in many respects. Such a life as hers has been. I do not wonder that she tries to hide herself from the cold world to live with her old age, her pets, her loneliness, and her pessimism. No wonder she has so much venom to vent. Although I feel that I could never be robbed of my hope and love long enough to write a poem as bitter as some of hers, yet I can see how she came to be such a hater of the world and individuals.

The poor old woman takes very kindly to me and seems to be happy when I come to see her. She has so little to cheer the monotonous days. I shall make it my business to see her as often as possible. It is a pleasure and a profit, too.

This is not a catalogue of my friends, only speaking of Miss Wilburn reminds me of a mutual friend of ours. It is Rabbi Fleischer, of Temple Adath Israel. He had a talk the other day in which you were one of the subjects, and Dr. Fleischer charged me to transmit to you his respects.

I am very sorry that you saw those verses but I am so glad to get your criticism that I can forget the regret. They should not have been published. The day before Mr. Hecht's birthday Mrs. Hecht asked me if I could write something for it. I was afraid for the publication. I never would have allowed it, not, perhaps, because I saw the faults in the poem but because I have been told so often not to let such hasty work go to print.

However I can forgive Mrs. Hecht, because she gave me a new opportunity to receive your criticism. It is amusing, though, what a scarcity of poetical critics in Boston, or a part of it, I have discovered. I would tell you what some people said of my poem but I do not wish to cast reflections on their literary judgement.

With thanks for your readiness to notice my "improvement," and with hopes to let you see more of it, I am

Your sincere friend

P.S. I shall study my French grammar with more enthusiasm hereafter in the hope of some day receiving a letter in that pretty tongue from you.

12. To Israel Zangwill [CZ]

123 W. 111th Street
New York, N.Y.
September 7, 1900

My dear Mr. Zangwill:

It was just like you to remember me in your letter to Mr. Cowen, although I had not written you a line for months. It is doubly a pleasure to write to you, always, because I know that I need not waste any words in excuses. I come to you knowing that you are not subject to the petty complaint of easily taking offence, therefore I need not physic you with apologies.

The most eventful summer I ever had is just coming to an end. I started out on it with determination to work and earn money, which, on account of poor business, we were badly in need of. I went as far as making an actual engagement, as interpreter between the Jewish patients and the staff of the Boston Floating Hospital. But Papa and most of my other friends objected, and made me break the engagement. Then I became private secretary to Dr. Grabau, the head instructor of the Bayville Summer School of Natural History, for three delightful, inspiring, profitable weeks. Rested, browned, noticeably healthier and infinitely wiser (I hope) I returned home from Bayville (Me.) to find things at home worse than ever. I now insisted on doing something to help, and got the superintendent of the Hospital to give me again the position of interpreter—he had not found anybody else. When I was ready to go aboard and begin in earnest, along came a new adventure to change all my plans. It was an adventure worthy of a storybook, and so deserves a paragraph to itself.

Mr. A. L. Murdock of the Murdock Liquid Food Co., Boston, had long been trying to take me under his guardianship. He is a very wealthy gentleman of seventy-two, who loves to advance poor people struggling for high ideals. I know through Dr. E. E. Hale, and Mr. Charles E. Hurd of the Boston *Transcript,* that he has educated or is educating at his expense a hundred girls, whom he picked out for some remarkable talent or another. Several of his "nieces," as he calls them, are writers of some note. When he proposed to become *my* uncle he wanted to do even more than he ordinarily does for his nieces. At first he wanted to adopt me altogether, but he soon saw that I thought my first and immediate duty to be towards my family, and would not be separated from them for a princedom. So he offered to be satisfied by making me his *first niece,* claiming the right, as my rich old uncle, to provide for all my wants from now onwards, to make life in general easy and pleasant for me, above all, every opportunity that money and experience can furnish for obtaining the noblest education a girl may be capable of utilizing. He offered to take all financial worries off my mind, to give me all the books and pictures I want, to let me travel with him—he travels much—whenever I could leave my books; he promised not to interfere in the plans laid out for me by my dear friends, nor in any way to exact the least obedience to his wishes when they were contrary to my mind or conscience, or to ask any return for what he should do for me, except the promise that I should regard half of all he had as my own, and him as the man who had my truest welfare at heart.

You may believe that I was a long time deciding how to meet these big proposals. I did not take all the responsibility, of course. I took into my confidence, with Mr. Murdock's permission—he always keeps his doings about his girls a secret when he can; he likes to remain in the background—I took into my confidence two trusted friends whom my father always consults about my affairs. It was decided that I ought to take advantage of the opportunities offered me. I promised to try it as an experiment, for a few months. The time has passed and I have discovered no reason why the experiment should not continue right on.

Because I do not wish to rise above my family more than a little at a time, just enough to raise them up gradually, I shall not take possession of my full heritage just yet. I make Mr. Murdock moderate his desire to see me live like a rich man's ward, and he is himself in sympathy with my idea enough to yield to my argument. I let him make me comfortable, but not more so than my folks. And I let him take me on interesting pilgrimages to historical or otherwise famous grounds, and buy me all the books I want, and in every way make it easier for me to accumulate the knowledge and culture I thirst for.

Mr. Cowen approves of my new relative, and this assures me anew that I did well to accept him. Mrs. Hecht's verdict I have yet to hear, as she and all the family are in San Francisco, which has for its centre of attraction Mrs. Sloss's baby girl—Mrs. Hecht's niece's own child.

The getting accustomed to the new and strange conditions has kept me busy and absorbed. Besides, I have been seeing many new things that imparted new impressions. I visited one of my earliest teachers, whose home is in the mountains of Vermont, and I studied New England village life while I dreamed and grew strong in the mountain air. Many other things I did, many experiences I had, that have made this summer very full and busy.

I am with the Cowens for a short visit. Next week school begins, and then back to books and study I go. Perhaps I shall write a little this winter. My mind is full of ideas, my head of impressions, that need some expression. I want to write some stories, but I am not sure—nor care—whether they will be the kind that are good to print.

Just now the freshest impression I feel is of the beautiful friendship and helpful attention of the Cowens. From living with them one short week I carry away a strength, an inspiration, a purity of soul that I get nowhere else. For what I receive from them all my rich uncle's bills would not sufficiently pay.

It is long since I had a word from you directly, yet I remember your suggestions about my style. I am beginning to feel conscious of the volume of this letter, and will stop to ask only before I close, that you consider how much I had to tell you and how long it is since I wrote to you.

My wonderful adventures must have entertained you, so I consider myself entitled in return to a few lines from you. I want to know what you think of my new situation, for even at this late hour I should wish to make any changes in it that you might suggest.

Mr. and Mrs. Cowen extend their kindest regards, as does also Mrs. Raphael, whom you knew as Miss Cowen. Adding my own sincerest greeting of friendship, I remain

Ever yours faithfully,

P.S. My new address is 6 Letterfine Terrace, Roxbury, Mass. We are half an hour's ride from Boston proper, in a clean, quiet, pretty place, where we have a more homelike home than we ever before had in this country.

13. To Israel Zangwill [CZ]

6 Letterfine Terrace
Roxbury, Mass.
October 7, 1900

Dear Mr. Zangwill:

Of all the kind letters you have written me, the last was one of the dearest. Your approval, advice, and correction are of unspeakable value to me. And I hold it a great privilege to be allowed an occasional peep into your own interesting life. Your letter gave me all these. Yet I was disappointed in it, and I am bold enough to say it, even after the first feeling is passed.

I missed something in your letter, just as I miss it in all the letters of all the wise people who write to me. No one of them is to blame. They do not know what I want because I never asked for it. Nor am I going to. You are the first to whom I as much as confessed the want which I will not name. It is because I expect so much more from you than from most men that I am to such an extent more open with you. And I ask, can't you say something to make me contented? Everything is dull and disagreeable, nothing is right. I cannot do right myself, because I am as much dissatisfied when I do so as when I do wrong. It seems to me nobody does what is right. I think nobody cares and as all is unright it is also unbeautiful. There is nothing interesting to do or see. Half the time I hate my books even, and would not do my lessons but that I hate explanations and investigations. Take away my studies, what have I left? I do not write, because every word I write one day sounds false the next. Perhaps all this that I am telling you is false. You will tell me so, if you know.

I laugh at the idea that you might think of my "good fortune" as the cause of my discontent. Perhaps you will say it has already spoiled me. That would be a natural way of reasoning, but it is not true. Nothing is true that is natural. At any rate, the world does not accept it as true. As to the truth of your theory, that I tried to anticipate, I can say only that my good fortune cannot spoil me if it does not, in the first place, make me feel elated. I only accept it, this wonderful good fortune. All the good things it brings me I only bear. For it is all as uninteresting and void of life as the rest of my privileges and actions under them.

You may say that I am petulant, hard to please, something of that sort. You are a master of English. You can easily think of sufficiently apt terms to describe me in my present mood. But I tell you, none of them will be true. I have a right, a sound right to be discontented. Yes, unhappy even, if I own to myself all the truth. Then can't you say something earnest to me? Are you unable, like everybody else, to say the one word I am waiting for? It is a pity for me to waste my time in displeasure. I would not do so, if somebody would tell me at least the reason of it all—why everything is dull and false and wrong.

Yours in all moods,

14. To Israel Zangwill [CZ]

6 Letterfine Terrace
Roxbury, Mass.
December 2, 1900

My dear Mr. Zangwill:

I am not going to answer your letter now. Perhaps I never shall. But I want to thank you for it, thank you as I never did before for anything you did for me.

Some day, when I am much older, when what I say will be accepted as the words of a soul that has lived and felt, not as the fitful utterance of a young heart just beginning to be conscious of life—someday you shall hear the history of my inward life during the last few weeks. Then will I answer your letter, if I ever do.

Your readiness in listening to my complaints and soothing me in my dark mood with kind words of advice and warning, will perhaps be rewarded in the fact that I am able to tell you that my life has already returned to the happy current in which it should naturally flow. It is even happier than it ever was before, and my renewed faith promises me greater happiness still for the future. At any rate, if trouble and sorrow come again, they will never be able to take from me the belief that the world is good at least, and that life can be made worth living.

I will close with a request. I want to have your photograph. I want it very much. You know that I never asked for it as others might, to have it to show to people as a sign that they have met the popular lion. I never would make a lion of my friend. I ask for your photograph because you stand for very much in my heart. I shall not ask you to write your name on it ever unless you feel particularly inspired to do so.

Gratefully your friend,

15. To Israel Zangwill [CZ]

New York, N.Y.
March 7, 1901

Dear Mr. Zangwill:

Shall I apologize for the shock I am giving you by letting this official heading announce to you without preparation that I have turned truant? Do forgive me; or rather praise me, for I have taken the shortest way to express the astonishing news of my staying in New York in this the middle of the school year.

The facts are these: my teachers and my physician having agreed between them that Mary Antin was "run down" and needed a change (unless she was willing to put up with nervous prostration later on), said Mary Antin packed her grip at once and made a bee line for 123 W. 111th Street, New York (as bee lines run with a steam engine ahead). This is the second week of the present visit, and letters arrived today in answer to a report of the patient's condition, prescribing a month more of The Cowens' Patent Cure.

Ask them what it is. They hold the secret. I can only grow strong and be happy and wonder at myself. I wonder also at the world—the beautiful world. I am learning many things with my books miles away, and grow more and more in love with the world and with men and women every day. Something else I am learning: my own weaknesses and powers. Is it not a wonderful thing, to look at yourself and *know* yourself? Did you ever do it?

I am very happy, because one lesson I have learned thoroughly: I can *wait,* and wait in peace. I know that

My own shall come to me.

So every night, when I look back on the day, I say, "I am glad I lived," and every morning, when I look ahead to the day, I say, "I am glad I shall live."

I am happy to rest and do nothing, as far as books and writing go. I am happy in the present and hopeful of the to-come.

Mr. Cowen said, when I asked him if he had any message for you, "I hope you didn't say anything bad about me." He has just added his "warmest regards," and to my remark that it took him a long time to warm them up he pinched my ear. Interpret for yourself.

Somebody with a long name is to call on us tonight, armed with the impression that he wants to meet me, and also with a copy of the December *Philistine* which does you so much glory, as Mr. Cowen informs me. It must be one of the *Little Journeys,* not the *Philistine* itself. But I shall be very glad to hear of you, believe me. Also I shall be more glad to hear from you, while I am recruiting at the Asylum, as I call 123, because they think I am crazy and yet they take me in.

With best regards, your friend,

16. To Israel Zangwill [CZ]

6 Letterfine Terrace
Roxbury, Mass.
May 21, 1901

Dear Mr. Zangwill:

This is a very late day for acknowledging your book, but my thanks are none the less sincere for having accumulated interest. Accept in addition my apology for this tardiness. I do thank you heartily and am really ashamed to have been so long in saying it.

More than a week ago I received through Miss Zirngiebel, Mr. Durland's friend, the message you gave him for me. It made me laugh, and it made me cry, and it made me wonder. I laughed because I was amused and pleased with your friendly threat, I cried because—I cannot tell you why, not yet at least—and I wondered whether you would think that my head does need any twisting around. There are some who do believe this, Mr. Zangwill, and they are in disease because my head refuses to be twisted away from the direction it faces obstinately.

There was a time, not so long ago, when I should have had no doubt as to the [illegible] you would take about this same obstinate head. Now I am never certain about anyone until I have brought him to the test. For there were one or two of my most intimate friends who took a stand exactly opposite to the one I had confidently believed they would take. I judged them by their ideals, and expected them to live up to their philosophy of life. But when the time came for me to reveal my soul, they condemned me, because I was true to it, because I insisted on practising as I preached while their fine theories were theories only!

Once I should have said, "Mr. Zangwill will be sure to think this way and do this and act so." Now I shall wait until you have expressed your opinion, and not presume to know it beforehand, merely because I happen to know your theories on certain subjects. I learn readily, you observe.

Yet I would throw away the warning of my experience with other men when it comes to you. I do not, I cannot believe that you would put away your ideals when the time came to make living truths out of them. You would not tell me, I am sure of it, that they must be consigned forever to the shadowy realms of mere speculation. You would say I am right in striving to *live* my ideals. I should not be disappointed in you as in those others. I am certain of this and if I should—well, you could no more twist my head than those who have tried before you. Come to Boston if you want to convince me of yourself.

If you were to come here soon, and if you were to receive me in a dusky room with an Oriental divan—do you remember the Sherwood in New York?—and if we were to get very confidential, *very,* I might tell you some stories that were never heard in a schoolroom. The fact is that I have been using some textbooks not prescribed by any school committee. Do you like stories, Mr. Zangwill? Do you like true stories?

It will not be very long before some of my stories will be published—not printed, but published. Then we shall hear some critics! No ink will be wasted, and "I told you so!" "What did I always say!" will be varied with a few more explicit comments. And you, Mr. Zangwill? I can rely on you for something original, at least.

You must not be troubled by my half-told tales. My conscience is in perfect peace, I assure you; and one of these distant days I will make my peace also with the world, and perhaps even with Mrs. Grundy herself. Conscience first, however—if one is brave enough.

If Mr. Loeb is still with you, please do remember me to him, and tell him that I was very sorry to have left New York without seeing his picture at the exhibition, particularly after my friend Miss Montagne, a Boston artist, praised it to the skies.

Although I was very glad to receive an autographed copy of your book in answer to my last letter, I should not complain if I had a little more manuscript next time. Perhaps I can make sure of my reward by sending you a list of Boston gossip across the seas. Another wedding in the Hecht family. Sally, Mrs. H.'s eldest single niece, will be married next week. The most moving item, to me (and perhaps it had best remain sub rosa), is that Mr. and Mrs. Hecht and the one niece remaining, "Little Lina," are going to desert the old house and take up their dwelling in a hotel. It makes me wish that apartments were not so fashionable. I prefer homes.

Next month examinations begin, so I must not let my books lie idle too long. Cramming? No, but I must work steadily.

Ever your sincere friend,

17. To Israel Zangwill [CZ]

The Harbor View
East Gloucester, Mass.
August 19, 1901

Dear Mr. Zangwill:

As I cannot imagine that dusky room and the soft divan in a public writing room of a seaside hotel, I shall trouble you with no more hints just now, but tell you the full story when I can. It may be very soon. For the present I want to say that of all your brilliant similes I consider the one in your last letter the most telling. Did you think when you made it, that it would go straight home? I hope you will not recall it until I am ready to remind you of it!

I do not think you will disown me, like most of my friends, when you hear my story. Oh, I cannot, cannot lose you too!—But I was not going to provoke your anxiety any more.

This summer has been a curious one with me. I have neither worked nor played much. I came down to study and sit for my portrait, expected to be done with the latter in a month, and go to the woods of Maine for the rest of the season. The portrait is not finished yet, as I was not in a condition for regular sittings, and but little of my planned work has been accomplished, because there are so many people here who know me that I cannot have much time to myself, no matter how plain I make it that I like to be let alone. I have to pay a high price for notoriety. Do you remember the surprised pleasure with which I showed you a Boston Sunday paper with a whole page devoted to my little delighted self? Oh, but I have out-grown my pleasure in fame of that sort! Often, when I was held up like a show figure by my proud friends (I give no names) and discussed as a piece of public property, subject to public advice and direction, I have wished that my little story had remained a harmless manuscript. Still, it is good to know that I have passed through the mill. I have gained through it much valuable experience, and my present happiness is indirectly based on that. I can afford to be grateful.

My most unpleasant experiences have not frightened out of me the wish to do great things with my pen. My mind is full of literary schemes, and during my longer sittings my swarming ideas slowly take their places in an orderly plan. I have a splendid theme for a Russian-American story characteristic of the present epoch, and it haunts me constantly, in vivid scenes and definite conceptions. I have also a subject for a long poem. (Do not be alarmed; I may never write it, or it may go out in the more harmless form of prose.) It sings in my brain day and night, in blanc verse, in [illegible], in every possible meter. At present I cannot write because I am living very eagerly. I cannot bear life's heart beat because it beats too loud. And I am going to write from life almost entirely.

I should like to see Mr. Loeb's pictures of "the most beautiful country in the world," and you, I think, would be interested in my friend Miss Montagne's pictures. Her boats and piers are true to the life of this salty old fishing town, and her portraits, which are her specialty, have each the individuality of the original. She portrays the spirit rather than the flesh. I wish she could do your portrait, both spirit and flesh. She is coming over to your side of the globe soon. I hope you will meet her and fall in love with her as I did, and then I could have my wish. Everything comes to me, you know. Beware!

Perhaps I *shall* come to Europe sooner than I used to plan. Are there any dusky rooms on your side? In either case, I shall remain, as long as you allow me, and even after,

Your sincere friend,

P.S. You may address me here until October.

18. To Israel Zangwill [CZ]

The Emerson
500 W. 121st Street
New York, N.Y.
October 8, 1901

Dear Mr. Zangwill:

I have something so good to tell you that I cannot wait now for the dusky divaned room. I am glad and proud to publish in broad daylight my marriage on the fifth of this month to Dr. A. W. Grabau of Columbia University. He has brought me to a dear little home near the University, where I shall take courses in literature and science in addition to other studies at home to prepare me for my life work. My plans are more glorious than ever, and my hopes of achievement are greater. With the inspiration of my dear Doctor's genius my own power will grow, till some day I shall produce a work for which you will be willing to speak as kind a word as you did for my humble firstling.

I have a great and noble man constantly by my side now, but I am still grateful for the friendship and help of those who have been kind to me, before I knew him and since, and hope that none of my old friends will think that I can spare them now. I want them all as much as ever, particularly since I have lost many to whom my marriage was displeasing on religious grounds. They might find these reasons unfounded if they could realize that I have not changed my faith.

Whatever your views may be, Mr. Zangwill, I hope I may continue to call you my friend as before. I am certainly unchanged except in name—

Your friend,

19. To Israel Zangwill [CZ]

The Emerson
500 W. 121st Street
New York, N.Y.
March 16, 1902

Dear Mr. Zangwill:

You probably did not expect an answer to your cordial letter of congratulation before this date, if you believe with the rest of the world that newly married people are selfish to all mankind, though angels to each other. I have my own opinion, but it is not to the point.

Do not say I was "prematurely" settled in life. I shall be nineteen in June! And my grandmother was married at thirteen. Talk about the good old times! The new times are better, Mr. Zangwill. I am sure no one woman in the old times ever had as much happiness as falls to my single share. The wonderful experiences whose effect you are interested in have opened to me new worlds of whose existence I did not dream when I met you. They have made me grow strong in many ways, so that what were once crushing burdens to me are now exercise grounds, so to speak, for my new capacities. The hard things of life do not make me pessimistic, but encourage my little attempts to help in the world's work.

In order that these attempts should be as fruitful as possible I am patiently devoting myself to my studies, although I burn to begin my actual

work. Your "little unconscious imp" stirs frequently, and yet the only freedom I give him is in short sketches on every subject imaginable, in connection with a course in English composition which I am taking at the
University. I am determined to keep him down until I am a little more
sure of myself. I am afraid that if I wrote now my ideas might run away
with me because I have so many. Moreover, I do not yet feel equal to the
managing of the ambitious plans which flash through my mind in moments of inspiration. To be more confidential, I want to write a *great
novel*. Keep it a secret. Only my husband knows it beside you and me, I
think; and neither of you know how wonderfully it is shaping itself. But
notice that it will be a *great* novel—or no novel.

The egotistic strain is not exhausted yet. Patience. You must hear about
my work. Besides composition (which is a curious study for me to pursue,
as I seldom accept other people's directions how to write in my own
style!), I am taking a splendid course in literature (Shakespeare, Brown-
ing, Tennyson, Matthew Arnold, with collateral reading) and one in
physics. These are special University courses. At home I continue in several languages with the addition of German, and mathematics. The best of
all, however, is my study of Nature, as a whole, under the guidance of my
own professor.

Now I can speak in the dual number. (How delightful to say "We" instead of "I"!) We are pleasantly situated almost on the University grounds,
where the atmosphere (in both senses) is congenial. We see few people—
the good Cowens are cold and polite—but we suffice for each other. However, Mr. Grabau threatens to take me out more and more to college
functions, as he holds an important position and must take a part in the life
of the institution. By the way, you could say something brilliantly funny
about this institution, which is situated on the former site of an insane asylum, some of the old buildings being still preserved. Give me to [illegible]
your next letter! But to return to my lord. He began here as Lecturer in
Palaeontology and in five months he has so distinguished himself as to win
the promotion to an Adjunct Professorship in the same science. May I not
be proud of such rapid progress? I am indeed now Frau Professorin!

You want to know more about my husband, and I want to know more.
However, the artistic sense (?) moves me to stop at this interesting point,
to keep up your curiosity till "our next." I read "S. Kohn & Son." All
right, but I am working out the problem, both in my life and in that of
one of my heroines-to-be, after a different model. I hope you will say "all
right" to me!

Your article on Zionism in *Leslie's* Christmas number I have not seen, but our good friend Mr. Lipsky has interested me in the movement by his individual presentation of the question. He takes a *universal* standpoint, and things appeal to me best from that vantage ground. I *doubt,* however, if I shall take an active part in the movement. I do not feel "called upon" to do this work, if you know the new application of this old fashioned phrase.

I see I have gone on after writing "The End." Well, this was a new story, and I had not written to you for a long time.

Write to me a little more than I deserve, for your letters are ever a pleasure to

Your quondam "schoolgirl,"

20. To Israel Zangwill [CZ]

527 W. 124th Street
New York, N.Y.
April 2, 1903

Dear Mr. Zangwill:

Once I kept up a regular correspondence with a young man, because I was conceited and thought I was doing him good. He was equally conceited, for he thought he was giving me pleasure. When I discovered that he was not a whit the better for my letters, nor I a whit the happier for his, I gently informed him that our correspondence was at an end. I have not heard from him since.

Why don't you treat me as frankly as that, Mr. Zangwill? Your not writing at all—and I am almost sure you owe me a letter—is no intelligible hint to me. You may simply be too busy, or you may think I owe you a letter, or you may have forgotten me. Still I do not know that you meant to close our correspondence. You must tell me.

No, I think I will tell you, and if I tell true you need only write me "yes"—or you can marconigraph it. Oh, I should like to get a marconigram; no matter what you say in it! But let me tell you whether you want to write to me any more. Of course you believed at first—*not* conceitedly—that you could do me good. What I believed does not matter here. But it has turned out that, with all your sponsorship and good advice and kind little interviews you haven't done me any very fundamental good; for I haven't had the grace yet to fulfil your prophecies—I have not published a book of lyrics, not a great novel, not even a good short study. So you see you have not done me much good, and you have done yourself harm; for your reputation as a literary judge must have suffered enormously as I recall our correspondence, you wrote me only to give me advice—to criticise my letters—to discharge your duty as my literary guardian. Am I much mistaken? So now that your kind ministrations have proved fruitless you ought to break off our correspondence. But you must do it formally, just as you would settle an account; for where I am concerned order is the best policy.

To be very serious now, I do not know if there is any reason why we should correspond any longer. Our lives are far apart—I do not even read your books and you haven't the opportunity to return the compliment. (By the way, don't you think I am wise not to read new books? It is a principle which allows no exceptions). To be sure there was pleasure for me in your letters, but a correspondence is not justified in these busy days by the benefit of one party only. And as I was the benefitted party in this case it was not for me to say the last word.

I wonder now why I wrote this at all. Perhaps because I am all alone this evening—Mr. Grabau had an important seminar to attend—No, I think I really wanted to know if I were still on your correspondence list.

Did you hear that Mr. Hecht died recently? "Little Lina" is the only one of the girls still unmarried. Mrs. Hecht must be very lonely. She sent me only a mourning card in reply to my letter of condolence. *She* doesn't want to correspond with me.

It is strange how my thoughts run on old friends tonight. It makes me feel as if I were still Mary Antin. Well, as far as you are concerned, at any rate, Mary Antin is the same as I.

Yours cordially,

21. To Louis Lipsky [AJH]

New York, N.Y.
November 22, 1903

Dear Mr. Lipsky:

I thank you and our other friend, the other secretary, for the honor of being "selected" for the special performance of גאָט מענטש און טייפּעל [*God, Man and the Devil*] which we shall attend with pleasure.

I am very glad that the Yiddish theatre will be brought before the extra-Ghetto world. May the play selected produce a favorable effect!

In addition to your heathen critics, I do hope you have chosen some East Side patriarchs and Americanized maidens to sprinkle the audience with an air of naturalness. But I have no doubt you have provided for all things perfectly, and I hope with all my heart (which is Jewish on Jewish occasions of this sort) that you will accomplish good things for the Yiddish stage by the first effort to introduce it abroad.

May I hope for a call from you and Mr. Richards between the acts? Our seats are Orchestra D17 & 19. If Mrs. Richards will be present, I should be happy to meet her.

Thanking you both for your courtesy,

Yours sincerely,

22. To Louis Lipsky [AJH]

80th Street and 11th Avenue
Brooklyn, N.Y.
December [?] 1905

Dear friend:

Your letter was like your return in person. The exchange of so much feeling and faith in such a brief correspondence after such a long silence is a new seal on our old friendship.

Yes, truly my heart is in Russia these dark days. My own blood cries to me, in fear of death, from Polotzk, from Riga, from Vitebsk, from Vilna, from Ekaterinoslav. See how these cities are scattered over the map of Russia, and judge how my heart is torn. At last accounts, my near relatives had all survived the murders; but this was weeks ago. The blood that then cried for rescue may now be crying for vengeance. And so it does, for my brothers and sisters were the victims in any case.

I see Miss Lazarus frequently. She has a wonderful consciousness of race, and she makes me feel that my Jewish descent is something that I must bear about consciously—something that I must account for every day I live. She stirs me in many ways. I wish you might know her. We often talk about you.

Come very soon. Oh, yes! do bring your dear friend, and I will hold her dear too. My husband, who is very keen about some things, wants to guess what you have to tell us, but I will not let him. I have not the least idea. You shall tell me.

Can you and Miss Schacht come to dinner on Saturday, the 23rd? We dine at half past six. It takes about an hour and a quarter from Brooklyn Bridge to our house. In your answer, tell me if you want directions about getting here.

If you cannot come on Saturday, come Monday evening. I cannot invite you for dinner that day, because I do not know how many Christmas guests my husband will bring me. My housekeeping is on a very small scale, of course. We should see more of each other on Saturday, when there will be no other guests.

Always yours,

23. To Louis Lipsky [AJH]   80th Street and 11th Avenue
                                             Brooklyn, N.Y.
                                             January 23, 1906

Dear Mr. Lipsky:

Tell me what you think of the papers I enclose—by letter, if you must; but I wish you would make this an excuse to repeat your visit. Can you and Hattie come to dinner or tea next Sunday (the 28th)? Dinner is at one o'clock. Tea at six. If it is a fair day, come early and see the country, and give me a chance to get acquainted with your future wife.

To tell you what I think of her would be so like making love to you that I am hardly bold enough to do it, though I am an old friend, and a married one. Dare I say it? Yes, I dare, for I can say "we," for my husband and myself. We both got a sure feeling, from our first meeting with your Hattie, that she is just the bright, sweet, soulful woman that you deserve!

Everybody I care for, among my younger friends, is getting married, which makes me very happy.

Don't lose my manuscripts if you can help it. I am my own stenographer, and I don't like copying.

"In Search of Summer" is the essay that was rejected by three magazines and admired by Mr. Gilder and some private friends. Would you advise trying that, or "Boulders," on the *Atlantic Monthly*? I like "Boulders" and wish it could be published.

Let me know about Sunday.

                                                      Your friend,

Thank you for the *Jewish Home*. But where are Rita Scherman's things?

24. To Louis Lipsky [AJH]   80th Street and 11th Avenue
                                             Brooklyn, N.Y.
                                             January 28, 1906

Dear Mr. Lipsky:

Thank you for lessening my disappointment in your not coming by sending me such a kind and prompt letter. Next Sunday we shall expect you ("you" is dual now—isn't that pleasant?) and we hope you will come long before dinner and stay long after. We shall go into town (N.Y.) in the evening. Perhaps we can all go together.

I am glad that you like my writing, but I am surprised that you thought the longest paper the best. I prefer the one about the Ice! But you will tell me more next Sunday.

You are very good to offer to place yourself between me and the displeasure or indifference of the editors. I gladly accept your offer. Send the paper you like to the *Atlantic,* only don't make yourself responsible for it (you have your own reputation to make!)—and let me pay the postage.

Mr. Grabau says I ought to introduce myself as the author of *From Plotzk to Boston.* I object. I want to conquer the editor by my own merits, not by the ghost of my former artificially puffed-up notoriety. Mr. Grabau says it would be a kindness to the editor to aid his discrimination by what is not in itself an unfair means, and a much practised method. I still object. It's a form of graft, if you analyze it a little. But he says—or Mr. Ward said that—Miss Lazarus's friend—that for the sake of the people who would be glad to see me on the stage, I ought to be willing to get there by the back door, if I cannot at first open the front door. Well, my convictions on the subject don't go very deep. It's just a little pride. So if you agree with Messrs. Grabau and Ward, you may overawe the editor by the magic of that phrase "author of" etc. I leave the casting vote to you.

My best regards to Eddie. (I thought it was Hattie.)

Yours as always,

25. To Louis Lipsky [AJH]

80th Street and 11th Avenue
Brooklyn, N.Y.
March 10, 1906

Dear Mr. Lipsky:

Ever a kind word, though a barren one, is acceptable when it comes from the *Atlantic Monthly.* "Mrs. Grabau" is greatly set up by the editor's desire of a chance to refuse her next article.

Why the *Ladies Home Journal?* Is it a refuge for the impossible in literature? I know that H. W. Mabie writes for it, but I don't worship Mabie. I should not be proud to appear in the *L.H.J.,* not cast down at being excluded from it. But I am sure you know best why you sent my paper there, and I admire your perseverance in sending it at all.

If it comes back this time, instead of sending it to the Boston *Transcript,* let me send it to my friend Mr. Hurd, who is still connected with that paper. I will take it off your hands from that point, and let you know the fate of it afterwards.

Eddie has not put in an appearance yet. I am waiting for her. These are fine days for walking.

With best regards,

Yours always,

Mary Antin in 1899

CHAPTER TWO

Toward *The Promised Land*

1910–1911

By 1910, the manuscript for *The Promised Land* was sufficiently advanced so that Antin and her daughter, Josephine, could accompany Grabau to London, Paris, and Scandinavia where Grabau was to take part in a geological conference. From there, they were to travel to Polotzk where Antin could proudly bring copies of *From Plotzk to Boston* to relatives still remaining in her native town.

One longs for Antin's impressions of Polotzk sixteen years after she left Russia under such difficult conditions. Alas, I have not been able to locate any letters or firsthand accounts of her visit. Doubtless, she would have been speaking Yiddish and verifying memories and impressions of life in the Pale. Was it possible for her to bridge the vast separation that time and circumstances had caused? Surely her relatives must have expressed their bewilderment or displeasure about her choice of husband and assimilated lifestyle.

While in Paris and London, she corresponded with Zangwill about her manuscript, which was in its final stages. Although she had great confidence in her work, she still solicited Zangwill's impressions and sent him the manuscript to read. He was the remaining friend of her former supporters, and Antin summoned his friendship from the past to help her now. From her response to his letter, it seems he not only read it as soon as he received it, but also, with minimal suggestions, encouraged her to trust her own judgment, which he valued.

On returning to New York, Grabau resumed his teaching at Columbia University, and soon the couple made plans to move to Scarsdale—considered then "out in the country." By spring 1911, the *Atlantic*

45

Monthly had accepted "Malinke's Atonement" and Antin was negotiating with Ellery Sedgwick about the magazine's serialization of her autobiography. She stipulated that it would also be published in a somewhat different and expanded version in book form.

Critics have written amply about Antin's antipathy to some Jewish practices as portrayed in *The Promised Land*. The evidence is there, especially as it pertains to the inferior position of girls and women in Orthodox households. She wrote eloquently about poor families who decided that it was preferable for girls to go without shoes so that money could be saved to educate the boys. Although examples such as this exist in Antin's work, other examples strongly express the pity she had for the abysmal poverty in which Jews necessarily lived because of anti-Jewish restrictions. She also clearly expressed the outrage and pain she felt about the bigotry and anti-Semitism that Jews experienced.

With the writing of "Malinke's Atonement" behind her, Antin returned to her serialized autobiography. The short story appears to have opened a wellspring of memories she needed to recount and record that would ensure a greater understanding of the Jewish immigrants' history. In June 1911 Antin began a series of letters to Sedgwick (thirty-six over a six-month period) in which she clarified her mission in writing the book. Employing Jewish imagery, she compared her task to being called up to the "bima" (pulpit) to read the Torah without error, the traditional sacred duty. "Since I am called to the forum," Antin wrote, "I pray that no error will pass my lips."* Although she often deferred to Sedgwick's suggestions, Antin held her ground when she inferred from his comments that he felt the book to be "too Jewish." She clearly wanted the Jewish element to be dominant and insisted that a handful of Yiddish and Hebrew words not be cut.

The letters to her editor are evidence of Antin's profound sentiments about her shared history with the Jewish people. They express the enormous responsibility she assumed in "getting it right," that is, telling an unprepared readership a history of the Jews that would evoke understanding, sympathy, and a warm welcome for the new immigrants. Although many years had passed since she was a girl in the Pale, her present life differing wildly from those days, Antin's memories were extremely vivid, and she committed herself to setting them down with the accuracy she believed they deserved. The passion with which she defended the inclusion of particular Jewish elements in the book and the anguish she exhibited

*Antin to Sedgwick, July 19, 1911.

over rendering the most faithful description of life in the Pale show Antin as one of our great chroniclers, in English, of Russian Jewish life in the nineteenth century.

26. To Israel Zangwill [CZ]

New York, N.Y.
May 31, 1910

Dear Mr. Zangwill:

I expect to be in London, with my husband and little daughter, for a short time in July. I should be very happy if I might see you and Mrs. Zangwill again. If it would interest you I would like to show you the manuscript of a book which I hope to publish on my return from Europe. You would be doing me an even greater service than you did in the past, when you said the word that enabled my friends to publish the story of my journey, if you would give me the benefit of your judgement on my present work.

Our address will be Care of American Express Co., 5 & 6 Haymarket, London, during our entire sojourn in Europe.

With best regards to yourself and Mrs. Zangwill,

Yours very sincerely,

27. To Israel Zangwill [CZ]

Inverness, N.B.
July 1, 1910

Dear Mr. Zangwill:

I should have made more haste to send for my mail, which waited in London while we wandered around the Highlands, had I known that such a cordial note from you was among my letters. It made me happy to read it, on a certain gray day when I confessed to a longing for a touch of real summer weather, such as we have in eastern United States.

We go from here to Edinburgh for a fortnight from the 8th—for the remainder of July, that is (Address, General Delivery). From Edinburgh to England, for the first half of August, but I cannot say just now where in England we shall be. My husband will complete his plans after we reach Edinburgh. The second half of August and part of September we shall spend in Stockholm, Mr. Grabau being a delegate from Columbia University to the International Geological Congress there. From Stockholm we have to go to Polotzk, if no epidemic, revolution, or other disturbance makes Russia unsafe at the moment. Polotzk is the most doubtful point in our plans, and on a visit to Polotzk depend my immediate literary plans. I wish just now that I had been born in a less uncertain country!

The fall and early winter we shall spend in Germany. We shall make ourselves at home probably in Berlin, where I mean to work on my book, which has suffered no revisions so far. How I had hoped to have your opinion before I settled down to work. It does not seem likely that we shall meet in August, but we shall make a second visit to England in January, I think, just before returning home. If, in the interval, you find time to read my MS, I shall put it into the best shape I can before sending it to you, and any suggestions you may make I shall receive with gratitude.

I hope all goes well with your [illegible] book. I almost envy you, being at home and at your work, although I never met anyone who enjoys travel more than I do.

With thanks for your kindness, promised and performed.

Yours sincerely,

28. To Israel Zangwill [CZ]

85, rue [illegible]
Paris
January 3, 1911

Dear Mr. Zangwill:

I shall be in London for about ten days from Jan. 6th. Is it possible for you to see me, and look over [illegible] manuscript? I ought to have sent you the MS in advance, but I have only one copy with me, and I thought I might find time to work on it. It is still incomplete, but I am ready to finish it now, as soon as I have settled some questions as to form and substance that have arisen. I hope you will forgive me for offering you an incomplete work, and give me your opinion and advice. The thing is so nearly finished that you will have enough basis for criticism, and it will help me greatly to think over whatever you may have to say, even if I am not able to adopt your ideas.

I am asking a great favor of a very busy man, I know, but I rest my petition on your friendship with a little girl of long ago. Our address in London is Care of American Express Co., 6 Haymarket. If you will send me word, perhaps I can send you the MS, by mail or messenger, as you direct, and call on you a few days later to hear your verdict.

If I should lose my MS between here and London, it will be a great pleasure to make an idle call on you and Mrs. Zangwill, if you will allow me.

Yours very sincerely,

29. To Israel Zangwill [CZ]   24 Tavistock Square
                                     January 9, 1911

Dear Mr. Zangwill:

I am very sorry to intrude upon you just when you are seeking a rest.
Ought I, in mercy, to stay away tomorrow, and send the MS by messenger? Selfishly I have decided to come. I do want to see you and it will be
for you to make our interview as brief as you should.

Our day of sailing has been postponed till Jan. 21; still that does not
give me time enough to get acquainted with London. I shall have to come
again soon.

Hoping to find you in good spirits,

Yours always,

30. To Israel Zangwill [CZ]   24 Tavistock Square
                                     January 17, 1911

Dear Mr. Zangwill:

I thank you for returning the MS so promptly, and for taking the trouble to write me.

Your remarks do not answer the questions I would have asked you if we
could have talked. I was not troubled about the publishing end: a few
people in the business told me I could choose my publisher. But you say,
or imply, that I can work out my own problems, which flatters me and
leaves me to my own wits. If anyone tries to give me advice after this, I
shall not listen, since I have your word for it that I know better than the
best critic what to do.

I agree with you about the "cousins and aunts" part. The whole
genealogical chapter needs to be rewritten. I hope you skipped most of
that.

You skipped too much in the middle of the story—I think it is the middle. (If I knew just what you skipped it would be a hint to me what to
leave out finally.) The titles you suggest seem to me to apply to the least
significant aspect of the story. I do not dare to tell you the title I have in
mind to use. It points out what I think to be the real moral of my biography, and you might be sorry to find how much you have missed!

You give me one very valuable piece of advice. You say "When in
doubt, cut." I know that to be good counsel, because it is so painful to
follow. And you shall be the first to benefit by my obedience. I was about
to add a number of things, but being in some doubt about them, I cut.

With many thanks for your kindness to me at all times, and especially now, I remain

Yours sincerely,

31. To Ellery Sedgwick [MH]

646 West 158th Street
New York, N.Y.
June 1, 1911

Dear Mr. Ellery Sedgwick,
4 Park Row
Boston, Mass.

Dear Sir:

Through Mrs. Charles B. Perkins I have received the manuscript of "Malinke's Atonement," which I hope to put into shape for you very soon.* I am preparing to move to the country and am too much interrupted just now to do good work. From the passages marked for cutting I gather your intention, but I cannot say till I have had more time to study the manuscript how far I am convinced. I shall do my best to satisfy you.

As I have one or two short things on hand that interest me, I may be tempted to go on with those before returning to Malinke, unless you wish to have it ready for an early number of the *Atlantic*.

Your comments on my work, passed on to me by Mrs. Perkins, have interested me greatly. Your praise, I must confess, flatters me, some of it surprises me. I can never know just what my Malinke or my Rösele looks like in your eyes, no matter how fully you express yourself, but what you and others have said does give me some idea of the figures my poor Jewish people make when standing detached from their overwhelming history, in the sight of a world that knows them but little. Malinke, to me, is Malinke with a thousand years of Jewish sorrows behind her, and a thousand years of empty hope. It is when I hear from my critics that I realize how little has been recorded of those centuries. I must by all means bear in mind the fact that not all things are in the reader's mind which are in the author's.

Thanking you for your kind interest, I am

Sincerely yours,

---

*Very likely Frances D. Bruen Perkins, who was married to a wealthy Boston art and music critic and organizer of cultural activities.

32. To Ellery Sedgwick [MH]   646 West 158th Street
New York, N.Y.
June 7, 1911

Dear Mr. Sedgwick:

Your letter of the 6th received, and contents taken to heart. I shall return "Malinke" very soon, trimmed, I hope, to your liking. Perhaps in my
first letter I sounded as if I meant to be obstinate. The truth is that I value
your advice, and I think I have the strength of mind to give in where it is
a question of my notions against your convictions.

I shall be glad of an opportunity to meet you the next time I come to
Boston. In the meantime I am sending you a couple of samples of my
book. And I can assure you I am not aiming at the pages of the *Atlantic
Monthly*. I am aiming, if you must know, at the heart of the world.

Very sincerely yours,

Address after June 13th: *Scarsdale, N.Y.*

33. To Ellery Sedgwick [MH]   Scarsdale, N.Y.
June 21, 1911

Dear Mr. Sedgwick:

I have your letter of the 19th. In a few days I shall forward the rest of
the manuscript of which you have read some portions, glad to think that
you are really interested. I am perfectly willing to forget that you are one
of the most important editors in the United States. You may be my friend,
foe, or acquaintance, as you like, as long as you are a critic.

I took a short journey into the country one day, and the green summer
closed around me. I can hardly find my way indoors, so used are my feet
to the fields and byways. But the tyrant conscience drives me to my desk,
insistently reminding me of a certain editor in Boston who once read a
story of mine with an *official* eye.

Very sincerely yours,

34. To Ellery Sedgwick [MH]   Scarsdale, N.Y.
July 5, 1911

Dear Mr. Sedgwick:

I return "Malinke's Atonement" today by express. If the changes I
have made do not satisfy your magazine judgment, please let me try again.

Several passages of one hundred words or more each, which you suggested might be omitted, seemed to me necessary or important. The number of Yiddish and Hebrew words I have reduced to a half dozen, and of these, two or three are not unfamiliar to English-reading people, if I am not mistaken.

With many thanks for your help, I remain

Very sincerely yours,

P.S. In your schedule of suggested cuts, I have marked in ink the number of words I succeeded in eliminating.

35. To Ellery Sedgwick [MH]

Scarsdale, N.Y.
July 19, 1911

Dear Mr. Sedgwick:

Late last night I sent you a telegram, accepting your offer to publish parts of my book in the *Atlantic Monthly*. This morning I write to repeat that I am greatly moved by your serious regard for my book. The late Charles E. Hurd of the Boston *Transcript,* after reading three or four chapters, expressed himself very much as you have done. So did Mr. Alonzo Rothschild, Mr. Ward, Mrs. Perkins, and one or two other friends; and there was one who prophesied the book to me years before I felt any interest in the subject myself.* But, although you were not the first to accept it as an attestation of American democracy, still your word is the first official guarantee that the people will listen to what I have to say. My friends will congratulate me on a literary success, but I have no mind for praise or approval. Since I am called to the forum, I pray that no error passes my lips. This is the only success I long for.

As soon as you return my MSS I shall go to work to arrange the first installment, according to your instructions. Is there nothing to bring you to New York at this season? It would be a great help to talk with you. There are a hundred matters to discuss, and a hundred more will arise. It is a pity to spend time on long letters. The question of the title alone will give me some trouble. I have hugged one phrase ever since the book was well along, but I am sure it is not suitable for a magazine serial. I must see how you arrange the material before I can hope to discover the proper title. Jacob Riis forestalled us some years ago, or we should find it plain sailing

---

*Alonzo Rothschild (1862–1915) wrote *Lincoln, Master of Men* (1906). He was the director of the Free Religious Association and a consulting editor on American history.

as regards the name.* "Americans in the Making" is a phrase that came of itself to your pen; but there is Mr. Riis with his "Making of an American." I really feel robbed!

Do you approve of my using the name Mary Antin (which you know is my own name) on the title page, and a different name—Esther Altmann, as I have it—in the text? I suppose you will divine my reasons for this transparent fraud: to take the edge off the boldness of my confessions. Almost all my heroes and heroines are living.

You speak of my inconsistency in mentioning some people by their real names and others by assumed ones. What do you consider the best form? Personally I should prefer to use people's real names throughout, but I am too lazy to write to everybody for permission. It seems absurd to mask the name of a man like Dr. Hale. His family approved of the passage concerning him. There is only one other person under a real name: my teacher Miss Dillingham, who died years ago, and whose family gave me permission to use her own name. The master of the Winthrop school was Mr. Swan; I call him Snow. I shall be grateful for your advice in this matter.

As to the publication of the book after you are done with it, I am inclined to be guided by your advice, knowing that it is based on a ripe judgment and a sincere interest in my literary welfare. My husband, Mr. Ward, and Mrs. Perkins, my three principal advisers before you came, had picked out the Houghton Mifflin Co., and Mr. Alonzo Rothschild had offered his services in the same direction. I am convinced that this unanimity of opinion points the way of wisdom, and yet I cannot but hold back a little when I stop to listen to the voices of two friends who said their last word to me more than a year ago. Mr. Hurd was in favor of another Boston house, on the ground that they were more modern in their business methods, and made greater sales than Houghton Mifflin. Dr. Hale never advised anybody to publish in Boston, but always urged authors to go to New York, for the best results. Knowing that these two were experienced in such matters, you will understand why I cannot easily disregard their advice.

In this discussion, of course I take it that publication in the *Atlantic* in no way limits my freedom in regard to subsequent publication in book form. The relation of the two publications I do not understand nor how the copyright is managed. I am content to leave everything in your hands, barring the opportunity to consider more than one offer of publication, if,

---

*Jacob August Riis (1849–1914) was a U.S. journalist and social reformer born in Denmark.

indeed, I have any. You have all my friends on your side, with the two exceptions named; but I like to feel that there is room for reconsideration.

You will not misunderstand my discussing the publishing house you favor previous to their taking any notice of my work. An offer from the aristocratic house of Houghton Mifflin will be only too great an honor for an unknown writer; and my gratitude to you for bringing me to their notice is in proportion. But I constantly forget my connection with the book. It is less my possession than a solemn trust. It is the fruit of my life, and my life was a gift from many givers. I must see that I render a sufficient account to them.

With many thanks for the time and thought you have spent on me, believe me,

Very sincerely yours,

36. To Ellery Sedgwick [MH]

Scarsdale, N.Y.
July 19, 1911

Dear Mr. Sedgwick:

In going over the proof of "Malinke," I find I have left a word in a form of which I am not certain. As I am far from reference libraries and advisers, I must trouble you to have the word looked up.

On galley 4 occurs the word *Ravs*, as a plural of Rav. I hardly believe it is the right form. It is very negligent of me to have let it go unverified to this point. The *Jewish Encyclopedia* may furnish the information, or you may have on your staff a Jewish authority. The forms of Hebrew terms in English have been subject to much uncertainty, unless I am the least informed of readers.

I have added a footnote—an explanation of the word *Rav*, on galley 3, thinking it helpful at this point. Do not let it stand if you think if superfluous.

Just as I was writing the mail was brought up, including a short manuscript returned by Mrs. Perkins. She thinks well of this slight story, well enough to have tried it on *Scribner's Magazine*. *Scribner's* has a different opinion, however, and now Mrs. Perkins wants me to try the *Outlook*. May I take advantage of your kindness and ask you to give me your opinion, before I waste any more postage stamps? It is such a trifle that I am ashamed to trouble you about it, but Mrs. Perkins's approval usually has something to stand on. You can tell me in a word if it is worthy of publication at all, and where it belongs among the periodicals.

Thanking you in advance, I am

Very sincerely yours,

P.S. Of course, if you think the article fit to publish, you need not return it to me, but send directly to the magazine you fix on.

Very sincerely yours,

37. To Ellery Sedgwick [MH]   Scarsdale, N.Y.
July 30, 1911

Dear Mr. Sedgwick:

I sent you about seventy pages of the autobiography yesterday, so as to reach you on Monday, but you will be disappointed, because the part that ought to precede what will be Chapter II of the book is not there. A condensation of what may be Chapter I of the book ought to open the story. I am working on it, and hope to send it to you in two days. If I understand your plan, that summary, with the substance of Chapter II, and possibly extracts from Chapter III, would make the first instalment. But I shall be guided by your advice.

The manuscript I sent you is in shape for the book—always liable, of course, to further revision. While considering the form you wish it to take for the *Atlantic,* can you also bear in mind the book form, and let me have the benefit of your opinion? It is asking a great service, but I know you are interested in the work as a whole. Mrs. Perkins was of the opinion that most of the chapters are too rich in incidents. If you have the same feeling, I must cut out more than I did in my first revision. It is easy to pick out passages not essential to the *story,* but besides the story there is a picture I am trying to make, and a lesson I want to teach. Perhaps I have too many motives!

I agree with you about the wisdom of signing all my writings with the same name. Do you disapprove of my using my own name on the title page (Mary Antin) and a fictitious name (Esther Altmann) in the text?

Other people in the story have been given names exactly in accordance with your advice: i.e., for all people except those unknown outside their private circles, the true names are used.

For the title of the story, how would this strike you? "Out of the Land of Egypt" or else "The Promised Land"? I have called the book "The Heir of the Ages" but I have been told it has not a challenging sound. I am not satisfied with the titles above suggested. I want to find a phrase that directly, in a word, tells what America does for the immigrant.

I hope you will not be much inconvenienced by having to consider the additional copy, when it reaches you, with reference to what you may have settled by that time. I found the time given me too short. That first part is especially difficult, because I know enough about the Pale to make a whole book, and it should be no more than a sketch; for the serial, perhaps only a hint. The American part is a simpler problem.

You have sent me several very helpful and considerate letters, for which I thank you heartily.

Very sincerely yours,

38. To Ellery Sedgwick [MH]   Scarsdale, N.Y.
                                           July 31, 1911

Dear Mr. Sedgwick:

The landing in America brings us to page *137* of my manuscript as it now stands, but the account of the journey is disproportionately abbreviated. Expanded it will take up another 10 pages, making the landing at about p. 150. If you had the complete MSS with you, you would see at a glance that the story of the voyage is too short. I summed it up in less than three pages, referring to my booklet *Plotzk to Boston* for a fuller account. If you have time to look through the booklet (W. B. Clark & Co., your neighbors, have it, or the Public Library) you may agree with me that the journey ought not to be slighted in the present story.

To the first 150 pages, you must add about 20, for the 1st chapter (missing so far). It will be reducible for your purposes, the same as the rest.

The MSS divides about this way:

Chap. I–V—*Russian* — 150 pp.

   "   VI–X—*American*—175 "

I understand that you want to use more of the American than the Russian material. You have very much the same idea as Mr. Alonzo Rothschild. He proposed that I sum up the whole Russian matter in one chapter (using the parts omitted for another work) and concentrate on the theme of the immigrant in America, calling the story "My Country"! It would make an intense story, but would leave *me* out of the book, and some of the best things in the book, if I am my judge, only count because they are true of an individual; namely, the author. But how would you like Mr. Rothschild's title? It reminds one of Dr. Hale.

Chap. I is going very slowly. I am praying for a spurt of inspiration.

I have two copies of the MSS. You can make reference by page to the part you have, if there is any occasion.

Very sincerely yours,

39. To Ellery Sedgwick [MH] New York, N.Y.
August 8, 1911

Dear Mr. Sedgwick:

I am in a panic at the idea of not revising my copy. I am sure you will find places in this chapter, the balance of which goes at the same time as this note, which are rough in structure and harsh in tone. I need not point out to you that in all this chapter we are on delicate ground. Anybody who is going to put in a plea for the Jew needs to choose his words most carefully. This part of the story ought to be told so that the reader should not have time to think between paragraphs. What I sent you is a first draft, of a portion of it. I did not even see the typescript, which was done by an inexperienced person. It is not my best work. Is it good enough for the *Atlantic?*

I take it very much to heart that I have kept you so uneasy about the matter. But I shall not bother you now with apologies: I assure you I did my best.

I thank you for your advice about my story "First Aid to the Alien." I shall let it lie for the present. Before the psychological moment arrives for presenting to the *Outlook,* I may find that I have outgrown it!

I look forward to your further communications about my work.

My husband, who is a very good judge, in the opinion of people not his wife, as well as in hers, does not approve of the title *My Country.* Mr. Rothschild meant it to be written with quotation marks.

40. To Ellery Sedgwick [MH] Scarsdale, N.Y.
August 9, 1911

Dear Mr. Sedgwick:

I thank you for your kindness and indulgence. I shall be content not to see proofs, if it must be so.

Yes, I am Mary Antin.

I am sure you will use most of Chap. I, all of which you have read by this time. I return herewith Chap. I complete (my spare copy). Please transfer my corrections to the copy you have blue-pencilled. And look out for the joining of the selections! In the MSS I read today the patching showed in places.

I judge from the way you treated the opening 8 pp. of Chap. I that you see the importance of a picture of the Pale as a background for the whole story. Many things in the later chapters really are not explicable without reference to the first part. How the figure of my father stands out against that background! I am sure it is not dull reading: the girl who copied Chap. I has already subscribed to the *Atlantic*! I hope you will not cut too much of Chap. I.

Now I am sure you cannot use in the first instalment more than Chaps. I & II. I have not had time to run through Chap III., but will do so this evening, and return it to you by the earliest mail out tomorrow. I hope I am not taking advantage of your kindness in sending me the copy to revise. Can the printers set up all the copy I send before the balance reaches you?

I have retained two Hebrew words, *rebbe* and *heder*, because they differ in connotation from their English equivalents. They occur so often that the reader will soon get used to them.

If you are inclined to cut out on p. 31, Chap. I, the paragraph about prisoners escaped from the Pale, I beg you to leave it in for the sake of Jewish readers—for the sake of my father. A great history is summed up in that paragraph. You will read it in my next book, of which my father will be the hero.

Sincerely yours,

41. To Ellery Sedgwick [MH] Scarsdale, N.Y.
August 9, 1911

Dear Mr. Sedgwick:

My letter of this afternoon will give you the impression that I am now satisfied with Chap. I as it stands, although it is little changed from what it was when I wrote so frantically about its faults. I am not satisfied; I am only resigned. In the future, it will be a good plan for me to write my book before it is printed! This haste makes my conscience sore. Jewish readers will reproach me for leaving out some of the most characteristic things in the picture of the Pale—the inner Jewish things. Neither did I use to the full the opportunity afforded one by Chap. I to answer certain popular criticisms of the Jew. I could have done so, without arousing any antagonism, if I made little Mashinke tell how such matters looked to her, in the manner in which she treats of other subjects. But when I went over the copy today I was too much hurried—and too much afraid to fill space. I shall make it all up in the book, but the *Atlantic* readers will be cheated.

I had the copy for only nine hours, on account of the infrequency of mail out here. There is no delivery; don't waste "special" stamps on me.

The only sure way to reach me in haste is by telegraph (via telephone from our nearest station).

If you see your way to let me see the proofs, after all, I shall be glad of the opportunity, and return them the same day, if they reach me in the morning.

I note your request for the next instalment for Aug. 28, and shall not fail you.

My husband still holds to his opinion that I should not use the name "Mary Antin" in the text. Mrs. Perkins agreed with him that the transparent fiction of calling the heroine by a different name from the author's would save some fastidious readers the shock of witnessing an absolutely unreserved egoistical revelation of the author's self. Some people do not care for Mary Johnson, as you know. If you see Mrs. Perkins soon, please ask her to convert you; or else you convert her, and then my husband will be outvoted. My own inclination coincides with your advice. I feel that my case is different from Mary Johnson's, for all I tell such intimate things in the later chapters (which perhaps are no longer clear in your mind.)

If you thought it sufficiently important to have a talk on these matters, and go over the balance of the MSS together, I might arrange to come up to Boston soon—say before Instalment II is due at the printers. My correspondent from Houghton Mifflin (whose name I cannot make out) asks for a meeting, but I fancy he is in no hurry. However, if you both between you can make out a strong enough case, I shall consider it my duty to meet you soon.

Very sincerely yours,

P.S. While condensing my MSS for the *Atlantic,* is it possible for you to think of the book to be, so that you can tell me, someday when it occurs to you, whether many of the passages you now omit ought to be retained later? Your omissions so far have been so justifiable that I have scarcely ever differed from you, but some passages I should be inclined to reinstate for the book.

42. To Ellery Sedgwick [MH]

Scarsdale, N.Y.
August 13, 1911

Dear Mr. Sedgwick:

On looking over the balance of the Russian portion of my story—Chaps. IV and V, which brings us to about the middle of the whole—and having in mind the portions of the opening Chapters you have marked for use, I come to the following conclusion, which I hasten to share with you in the hope that it is not too late for you to be guided by it.

The really important things of the Russian half of the story are told in the first two chapters. Chap. III, dealing with the heroine's childhood in a rather poetic way; and Chaps. IV and V dealing with the heroine's education and spontaneous intellectual and moral development, in an interesting but expansive manner—all three, some 95 pages, (typed) can easily, and without loss of important details, be condensed to the bulk of one instalment.

If you are willing to give the Russian story so much space, make *two* instalments out of Chaps. I and II, and a third of Chaps. III, IV, and V combined. Looking ahead to the American Chapters, I think the last (X) may be entirely omitted, a summary of it—the moral, so to speak—being inserted *before* Chapter IX—a very dramatic Chap. (now called "A Kingdom in the Slums") which is worthy to close the serial. That leaves of the American Chapters (V–IX) about 160 page to be used, to make, as you originally planned, three American instalments.

To give you some confidence in my judgment, I will tell you that Mrs. Perkins, who discussed my work with me at length, considered that I had a good perspective of my own work.

I hope it is not too late for you to make use of this analysis of the material, if you feel inclined to do so.

My husband, who is my counselor and guardian, wants me to ask you to see that my true name (Mrs. Grabau) is not divulged in connection with my writings, whether for advertising or any other purposes. It is my intention to return to Russia for further studies within two or three years, if not earlier, and he thinks that the author of words so unfriendly to Russia as some of mine may find herself hindered by close surveillance, or worse, in any attempt to reenter Russia under her known name. As nothing is too insignificant for the Czar's watchdogs to spy upon, my husband's counsel of caution had better be observed. The Czar will not feel the throne tremble beneath him because a former subject of his makes a complaint against him in a strange language, before an audience of several thousand foreigners who have no power to chastise him; still the wife of Prof. Grabau, a Christian American citizen, will have less trouble about passports and other official matters than the Jewish authoress of naughty sentences.

I shall send you very soon the balance of the Russian material, so as to keep well ahead of the printers.

Very sincerely yours,

43. To Ellery Sedgwick [MH]   Scarsdale, N.Y.
                                                    August 18, 1911

Dear Mr. Sedgwick:

I leave my ancestor Israel Rimanyer in your hands. My judgment of particular passages may not always be the best guide in making up the copy, because your greater experience will better tell you what the total effect will be on readers who have not in their minds the parts of the story yet to come, or to be omitted, as I have them in mind. After I have expressed my views as strongly as I could, I am content to leave the ultimate decision to you.

The word *cheder* should in every instance be changed to *heder,* as in "Malinke."

I am grateful to you for the care you took to have my true name struck from the plates. I must try to get all my suggestions on record betimes, so as not to put you to unnecessary trouble.

I am preparing the copy for the next instalment (which you will receive during the week) in the expanded form to be used for the book, according to your original directions. Of course I expect to see the greater part, instead of the lesser, of these chapters blue-pencilled.

I enclose a draft of the description of the autobiography you asked for. Do make me recast it if it is not what you wish. I have no idea how to write an advertisement.

How about a title? What is the name of the book described in my paragraph? Have you no use for the general title of the several instalments? I am as curious as an outsider.

Yours very sincerely,

P.S. My "Word to my Fellow Citizens" might be a better introduction to the book than the original one, especially if "My Country" is used as the title.

44. To Ellery Sedgwick [MH]   Scarsdale, N.Y.
                                                    August 23, 1911

Dear Mr. Sedgwick:

I received today a check for $150.00, for which I thank you.

I notice that the note accompanying the check refers to my contribution under the title of "Autobiography of Mary Antin." I suppose that is just a handle for the business office, as no such title was discussed.

I am glad you like the "editorial note." I am coming to your office some day to ask you a great many questions. The machinery of magazine making is beginning to interest me.

A neighbor of mine saw "Malinke" very attractively advertised in the public Library. Being acquainted with my brother's name, he promptly charged me with the authorship; whereupon underneath my blushes, I felt a distinct stirring of gratified vanity. So much for my noble missionary motives!

The copy you want is escorted by this note.

Very sincerely yours,

45. To Ellery Sedgwick [MH]   Scarsdale, N.Y.
                                               August 1911

Dear Mr. Sedgwick:

I am sending you Chaps. IV, V, and VI, which takes us well beyond the landing in America.

You will find two forms of the story of the exodus—one too short, and one too long for you, I think. If you like the longer form, it can easily be cut down by omitting or abbreviating some of the quoted passages. The quotations are from my *Plotzk to Boston,* published in Boston in 1899. If you do not like the long form of the story for the *Atlantic,* perhaps you will approve it for the book. My fear is that it is too interesting for a single episode. As I heard it read aloud just now, I forgot everything that went before—even I, to whom it is an old story.

In the present batch of copy the family name occurs for the first time. I have used *Antin,* in deference to your advice, but my family are not convinced of the necessity of giving us all away. Before the name is actually put into type either you or they will come around to the opposite view. My own instinct is to tell all and say "this is a true story," but my people surely ought to have a vote in this case. And remember that my husband and Mrs. Perkins, two unprejudiced judges, advise the use of an assumed name in the text as a matter of taste.

May I trouble you to have one copy of Chapter I returned to me? It was sent you in duplicate, all except pages 1–8, of which you have only one copy.

Very sincerely yours,

46. To Ellery Sedgwick [MH]   Scarsdale, N.Y.
                                                   September 3, 1911

Dear Mr. Sedgwick:

I am thankful that the more important of the two packages of manuscripts you sent suffered no harm in the accident. The damaged package
has not yet reached me—things are a little slow in Scarsdale—but whatever condition I shall find it in, the mischief is not so great. I shall have to
have a copy made from my original, which I have safe up to this moment.
The bill for damages will amount to the stenographer's charges, on my
side; but the express company ought to pension you for the worry the accident caused you.

You will not receive the revised MSS until Tuesday, on account of the
holiday Monday. I took only twenty-four hours to go over it, but I have
done it very thoroughly. Still, I should be glad to see the proofs, if time allows. The printed form always shows up errors, as you know.

You owe me no apology for cutting the manuscript. I never hope to en-
counter a more considerate blue-pencil than yours. The wonder is that you
have so much patience with the frequent sermons in my pages, when you
read with one eye on the lazy subscriber. With the exception of a few short
passages, your cuts eliminate nothing that it troubles me to see pushed out.
My pet paragraphs you seem to regard with the same respect as I do. I have
nothing to complain of. On the contrary, I am very grateful.

It looks to me as if the copy I am returning, even in its emasculated
form, will be too much for a single instalment. (I have no idea how long
the first instalment turned out.) I have marked a number of passages for
further elimination, subject to your approval. The passages I mean are enclosed in pencil brackets with a cross [✗]. I must also ask you to look out
for marginal notes I made where I was in doubt. I wish I could spare you
these details, but I am not wise enough to arrange the copy without your
help.

A last word about names:

I shall keep to the name "Mary Antin," and we agree to try and keep
my identity a secret.

The name "Hirsch" does not exist in the manuscript any more, or it
should not. I meant to cut it out—yes, I know I did, before sending in any
of the MSS for the printer. Hirsch was my grandfather's *middle* name—
Joseph Hirsch Antin—but as surnames were not used, it became conspicu-
ous, and misleading. As soon as I realized that it was puzzling you, I cut it

out altogether, and it is no loss. There are plenty of dreadful names without the unnecessary ones. Antin is and always was my father's family name.

If you would have a set of proofs of Instalment I sent me, it would be helpful to me in revising the rest of the MSS. I do not know what you made me say in the beginning of my story, so I am afraid incongruities may creep in, unless I have that to refer to as I go along.

I have material for Instalment III ready. You can have it whenever you wish.

I was pleased to see "Malinke" in the latest *Atlantic,* but it frightened me to see how much room she took up. My enterprising neighbor, who found me out as the author of "Malinke" through knowing my brother's name, assures me that I am getting my share of advertising. Indeed, I found p. 31 of the current *Atlantic* very fascinating reading, and my neighbor tells me I ought to feel flattered to have my story "featured" so prominently. As the gentleman is himself an author, of far greater experience than I, I cannot but take his advice and feel flattered!

I do not know to what department to send my thanks for the generous present of two copies of the *Atlantic,* so I put them in here, hoping that you will turn them over to the proper office.

Very sincerely yours,

47. To Ellery Sedgwick [MH]

Scarsdale, N.Y.
September 28, 1911

Dear Mr. Sedgwick:

By the first of next week you will receive the final chapters of my story. Hew away at it to your heart's content! I have grown callous to the process.

You remind me, in your letter of the 27th, that the career of the *Atlantic* will not end with the last instalment of my serial. I would not be an editor for any bribe. Plans are chains of slavery. I have no plans whatever, unless irritable things in my head can be called plans. Do not count on me, if you value your peace. On one condition only would I dare to promise you specific things at a specific time: that is that you should bind yourself to supply me with *cooks* as fast as they leave me. I am a woman, Mr. Sedgwick, living in the country up to the eyebrows in the servant trouble. Ask Mr. Greenslett, who saw some evidences.* The fate of the *Atlantic* is less in my hands than in those of the cook.

*Ferris Greenslett (1875–1959) was an editor and author and from 1910 to 1962 was the director of Houghton Mifflin.

I am flattered to learn that Rabbi Fleischer, the much talked of and much talking, expressed some interest in me. But I do not know what can be the root of his sudden interest. When I called on him by appointment, a few months ago, he did not care to learn what I had done with my life in the ten years since we had met. He spent the whole hour showing me pictures of himself. If he is a friend of yours, I apologize for being impressed with his colossal vanity. For your sake, I will forgive him for finding me least interesting when present.

Very sincerely yours,

48. To Ellery Sedgwick [MH]

Scarsdale, N.Y.
October 5, 1911

Dear Mr. Sedgwick:

I am waiting for proof, and thought it best to let you know that I have received none, lest another accident lurk in the pause. Perhaps I have miscalculated the time. I think it is the December instalment that I last revised. I have all the rest of the copy ready to send whenever you wish.

The first instalment was very interesting to me, as I had not seen it after you did things to it. I intend no reproach when I say I detected the patchwork in places. Very likely it was only my knowledge of the omissions. A few errors that could be laid at the door of the proof reader also hit my eye, but then I am sensitive in this case. I have had plenty of evidence that the story reads well enough to all outsiders. Your clipping from the *Transcript,* for which I thank you heartily, is not all I could have hoped for; it is a great deal more. Indeed you will prove a true prophet if this first fragment, gotten up in such haste, can so impress a Boston editor.

Several times you have asked me about my future work. I have not replied because my answer has to be a blank. I have nothing to show you at present—nothing on paper. My head is full of Polotzk. Can you feed your readers more Polotzk? And in any case I am not a person to be counted on. I do not think I can turn out stories or anything just because they are wanted.

I shall be very grateful if you will have all of my manuscript returned to me after you are done with it.

Very sincerely yours,

P.S. I enclose a bill for damages against the express company who chewed up a part of my manuscript. Kindly forward it to the guilty parties.

49. To Ellery Sedgwick [MH]   Scarsdale, N.Y.
                                                   October 11, 1911

Dear Mr. Sedgwick:

My father calls my attention to the fact that the *Boston Advocate* is reprinting my autobiography. I do not know whether this is an act of piracy, or whether it is all according to publishers' etiquette. I have no objection to the story being copied any number of times, if my devoted publishers see no harm in it to our mutual interests. I only thought it fair to warn you, in case the timing is of any consequence, in your judgment.

You will not find it easy to locate the *Advocate* in the journalistic *Who's Who*. It is a harmless toy weekly, with an editorial and contributing staff three or four strong, if I am not mistaken; devoted to Jewish interests, and doing nobody any harm. I don't believe more than three hundred people are in the secret of its existence. As a Jew, I would feel like apologizing for it, if it were of sufficient consequence. My father's zeal is due to his opinion that my story does the little sheet too great honor! For my part, I think it a fair free advertisement.

The book is so nearly off my mind that my old stories begin to buzz in my brain. I love my stories, the untold ones.

Until I learn what your copyright (the Atlantic Company's, I mean) covers, I shall have to ask you questions. Who has the right of granting permission for translations? A lady in Texas wants to translate "Malinke's Atonement" into Yiddish. I should raise no objection, but should insist on editing the translation. I know Yiddish well enough for that. If you wish to communicate with the would-be translator, I can get you her name and address, at this moment unknown to me. The request came through my sister.

                                                   Very sincerely yours,

Amadeus Grabau, c. 1930

CHAPTER THREE

U.S. Politics and Zionism

1912–1916

The enthusiastic reception of the *Atlantic Monthly*'s serialization of *The Promised Land* transformed Antin into a public figure. She wrote articles for various journals and developed a very successful public-speaking career. One of her articles, "A Woman to Her Fellow-Citizens," promoting Theodore Roosevelt's Progressive Party candidacy, caught the former president's eye. Chiding the restrictionists who sought to limit immigration, Antin wrote, "It's hardly fair to call immigration a burden before a consistent [n]ational effort has been made to turn it into a resource."* Roosevelt responded in kind by proposing they meet at the *Outlook* offices. That meeting was the beginning of their friendship and correspondence. Roosevelt was very taken by the twenty-nine-year-old Antin and was soon enthusiastically arranging to have his new daughter-in-law's mother meet her (appendix, letter 1). Antin, in turn, became a great admirer of his and was rewarded by the inclusion in his intended autobiography of her photograph. He wrote Antin acknowledging her profound influence on his thinking and affirmed her rightful position among noted Americans. "I want your photograph simply as I want the photograph of Jacob Riis and Jane Addams . . . my dear Mrs. Grabau," Roosevelt wrote (appendix, letter 2).†

In her new role as a celebrity, Antin and her autobiography became frequent subjects in the press. Articles appeared praising *The Promised Land* and holding her up as an example of an American success story. Politically, liberal groups and Jewish organizations sought the increasingly popular

*Antin 1912d.
†Roosevelt to Antin, undated.

writer to express her views in furtherance of their causes. Demand for her lectures became so great that she engaged a management company, the Players, to organize her speaking tours and hired a press service to collect and preserve newspaper articles reporting on her many talks. She used her newfound fame to promulgate her political and ethical positions, culminating in 1916 with her position as chairman of the Women's Committee of the National Hughes Alliance. The alliance promoted the Progressive Charles Evans Hughes as the Republican Party candidate for president, and Antin traveled across the country with other prominent figures on the Women's Campaign Train, giving speeches in major cities.

As the wife of a Columbia University professor, Antin became acquainted with the political activists and thinkers of the day. Among them was Randolph Bourne, a recent Columbia graduate and noted pacifist and essayist with whom she corresponded.* Although she admired his essays and valued his company, Antin did not publicize her own attitude toward World War I. Only later, in reading a letter to the writer Mary Austin (1868–1934) about Antin's suffering in the face of her husband's pro-German attitude, does the reader understand why there is no mention in her letters, nor is there any public expression of her views, concerning America's eventual entry into the war in 1917.

In 1914, in response to her increasing alarm at the national sentiment to restrict immigration and in reaction to the prevalent anti-Semitic and antiforeigner atmosphere in the country, Antin wrote *They Who Knock at Our Gates: A Complete Gospel of Immigration*. The book proposes a humane immigration policy, comparing the early-twentieth-century immigrants' hopes and the worthiness of their efforts to the Pilgrims' experience of leaving their native land and coming to America. The travails of these immigrants are in turn likened to those of their biblical predecessors, the Hebrews' exodus from Egypt and arrival in the Holy Land.

They Who Knock at Our Gates was not as well received as *The Promised Land,* which was one of the most popular books of its day. The autobiography had brought Antin financial security and social standing. She frequently hosted celebrities in her home and was famous in her own right. The income from the first book provided enough money to send her daughter, Josephine, to an exclusive boarding school. As a public speaker she focused primarily on the question of open immigration, increasing her

---

*Randolph Silliman Bourne (1886–1918), an essayist and philosopher, wrote *Youth and Life* (1913), a collection of idealistic essays, and later published works on philosophy, education, and literature. He was physically deformed because of a childhood accident.

efforts in rallying opposition against restrictive legislation. Her position was unshakable. Following a speech in Colorado Springs, the blue blood Ruth Woodsmall confronted her in a scathing letter (appendix, letter 5).* Woodsmall alleged that Antin was ungrateful to America "who has given you everything" and whose life's fabric would be destroyed if "all who knock at her gates shall be admitted."† Antin remained undaunted and unintimidated, supporting her point of view with very persuasive language. Her passionate adherence to an open immigration policy would be her credo throughout her public life.

Although Antin felt that her primary work was to promote open immigration, she developed an accompanying theme to many of her talks: support for Zionism. The year 1914 was defining for American Zionism. Until then most Jewish groups—the Orthodox who believed Zionism to be antireligion, German Jews who feared it would compromise their standing in American society, and the socialists who considered it a threat to their ideology—all opposed Zionism. But when the respected Jewish American lawyer Louis Brandeis influenced other Jews of intellectual and personal stature to join him publicly in support of Zionism, the sentiment of many American Jews changed forever. Among these intellectual Jews who now spoke out in support of a Jewish homeland was Mary Antin.

Someone who shared many of her views and whose background was similar to hers was Horace Kallen. Kallen had also come from Europe as a youngster with his family and, like Antin, had broken with Orthodoxy. He later proclaimed himself an unbeliever, a statement that cost him his English teacher's position at Princeton in 1905. Later, in 1918, his pacifist leanings during World War I caused him the loss of another position, this time from the University of Wisconsin. Antin was drawn to this Jewish intellectual who renounced Judaism's religious aspect but was a tireless worker for Zionism and social causes.

Kallen believed that the Jewish people needed a home in Palestine to protect them against persecution and to enhance their cultural heritage. His thinking had a great influence on Antin. It was he who suggested that she attend the 1914 Conference of American Zionists in New York, an inspirational event for which she later thanked him gratefully. Their correspondence covered a wide variety of topics: from politics and literature to Zionism. Their mutual admiration prompted Kallen to propose that Antin

*Ruth Frances Woodsmall (1883–1963), a descendant of the first English settlers, was educated at the University of Nebraska (B.A. 1905) and Wellesley College (M.A. 1906) and became general secretary of the World YMCA (1935–1947).

†Woodsmall to Antin, Feb. 20, 1916.

give a series of lectures at the University of Wisconsin, and she invited him to Scarsdale for a Hanukkah party with a promise of homemade potato pancakes for which she used the Yiddish word and script.

Kallen was part of the Zionist circle of friends and acquaintances that included Jessie Sampter and Henrietta Szold.* The friendship with Kallen allowed for the occasional heated argument, whether over politics and Antin's affectionate respect for Theodore Roosevelt or over what she perceived as his passivity in the dissemination of Sampter's writing. Antin and Sampter met as young women at Zangwill's New York home, and together they visited Josephine Lazarus regularly. The two young women discussed going to Palestine together, but only Sampter went. Their friendship continued despite the separation of distance and time when, years later, Sampter defended Antin against criticism that alluded to her alleged anti-Jewish feelings. After Sampter settled in Palestine, she instructed her sister to discard all her papers except for Antin's letters.†

Antin's Zionist talks softened some of the criticism against her assimilationism. She argued that "assimilation is going on in every land where social equality is guaranteed by law"; however, she yearned for the time "when we [Jews] have the protection of a home center behind us . . . and when the precious seed of Jewish culture is safely embedded in a national core."‡ Antin believed that assimilation was a matter of choice, but it in no way abrogated the Jewish people's right to a homeland.

50. To Theodore Roosevelt [LC]   Scarsdale, N.Y.
                                          December 4, 1912

My dear Colonel Roosevelt:

My excuse for enclosing the accompanying announcement is a phrase that you dropped yesterday during the discussion on immigration. "Especially the girls," you said, speaking of the necessity of looking after the immigrants after they are admitted. You will be glad to know that the Council of Jewish Women is doing an important work in looking after immigrant girls. It was in my desire to get more people interested in this truly patriotic service that I allowed them to put me down for a talk at the

---

*Jessie Sampter (1883–1938), a poet, writer, and Zionist, was one of the founders of Kibbutz Givat Brenner. Henrietta Szold (1860–1945), a prominent Zionist and founder of the women's Zionist organization Hadassah, was a pioneer in Israel in many fields, including education, social work, and medicine.

†Badt-Strauss 1977.

‡Antin 1917, 5.

meeting to be held on Sunday, this being my first infringement of my rule of silence in public.

I wish you were going to be at the meeting, to say "especially the girls."

For Mr. Grabau and myself, I thank you for the pleasure of yesterday's meeting. It did us both good to see the Chief of the Progressives so full of life and plans. We shall pass the word along that the Chief bids us be of good hope.

Sincerely yours,

51. To Theodore Roosevelt [LC]

Scarsdale, N.Y.
December 10, 1912

Dear Colonel Roosevelt:

I am profoundly grateful for your thoughtful courtesy in sending me a word in time for that meeting on the immigrant girl question. I quoted it as a proof of the fact that the necessity of looking after the unprotected foreign girls was looming up in the minds of people who have much to do with shaping our immigration policies. It made a point, I can assure you.

Very gratefully yours,

52. To Maude Elliott* [BU]
December 12, 1912

My dear Miss Elliott:

The book you asked for goes to you by the same mail as this, and with it my best wishes for the prosperity of the Progressive cause in Rhode Island and elsewhere. I have written my name in the book as you request, and a sentiment that is often heard from the lips of Russian Jewish immigrants. Tell the person who acquires the volume that if any difficulty is experienced with the last line of the inscription, the first Jewish rag-and-bottle man who disturbs your afternoon nap may be called in as an interpreter.

Sincerely yours,

*Maude Howe Elliott (1884–1948), daughter of Julia Ward Howe and Dr. Samuel Howe, noted abolitionists, was acquainted with famous writers and philosophers from a young age. Elliott had a successful literary, journalistic, and art-critic career and in 1912 became a founding member of the Progressive Party. She shared with Antin an ardent devotion to Theodore Roosevelt: "I would have died for Roosevelt without a thought," she said.

53. To Randolph Bourne [CU]   Fox Meadow
                                         August 11, 1913

Where are you now, dear Mr. Bourne? If you are happy somewhere in Europe, it is good for you, but not for me. I would like to know that you are nearer, near enough to go for a walk with me.

For the first time since that autumn day when you came to Scarsdale, I find myself on the road we took through Fox Meadow, to Hartsdale station. I have thought of you often this summer, though I gave no sign. I have been marking your essays for rereading, and telling people what good things I have found in them, and wishing to talk to you about them. This morning as I turned into the meadow, and saw the ripe grasses rippling in the sun, and the wind leaping in the shining oak, and the shadows moving in masses between the tree trunks, I thought of you, and felt a pang of loss, remembering the weeks I have allowed to slip by without trying to see you and talk with you. I thought of you not merely because you were my companion the last time I visited the meadow, but because the wind and the shadows and the dancing grasses partake of the high mood of a clean, blue summer morning; and so do you, in your book and out of it.

When you come back, I hope you will make me an early visit. You will have to write, or call on Prof. Grabau, to get directions for finding us. We have got away from the main road, and live on the crest of Murray Hill, nearer the Hartsdale Station, and the farther end of the meadow.

I came out here to work, not to write letters. Shall I be able to forgive you for projecting yourself into the landscape, when I meant to feed my muse on solitude? Or would you say that friendship is as great a thing as work? You could easily persuade me of that. I have often felt that the utmost I can hope to achieve by my writing will fall far short of what I can get out of life by just living. Writing is not itself a part of life to me. It is only a transcribing of finished adventures. *Everything* I write is autobiography. Does it pay? I might be discovering new worlds all these long mornings when I write, instead of sitting still to tell about the worlds I have already visited.

But two or three editors are waiting. I must to my reporter's task!

All good wishes to you wherever you are. Is it a new book you will bring back with you?

Yours in the joy of living,

54. To Theodore Roosevelt [LC]
Box 195
Scarsdale, N.Y.
August 29, 1913

My dear Colonel Roosevelt:

I am only too proud to be included photographically in your book, on terms of perfect understanding. I shall forward the desired photographs to Macmillan's at once, and when the book comes out I shall turn the pages without reading till I come to that very picture, or I am very much mistaken about my feelings.

Since circumstances provided me with an excuse for writing to you at this time, I cannot refrain from expressing my utter delight in your last autobiographical article in the *Outlook*. In our house, we have been saying of the successive installments "This one is the best yet!" But now this last one—it really reaches a climax of excellence! Its directness, its humor, the inevitableness of its moral—they are entirely yours. I wish I could make all your enemies read your autobiography. You would then have the whole world for your friends. With best wishes for your every enterprise, from Mr. Grabau and myself.

Sincerely yours,

55. To Rabbi Stephen Wise* [AJA]
Scarsdale, N.Y.
September 14, 1915

My dear Dr. Wise:

I never had an offer of hospitality proffered in such modest fashion as does your friend Rabbi Cronbach, in the letter you were good enough to pass on. Certainly I shall be glad to be taken care of by Beth El people; and if lots are to be drawn, I hope the family that is most remote from car tracks and other city noises will adopt me.

Of course I do not know at this time how much or little time I shall have in South Bend. Sometimes there is only time to alight, say my say and be off again. If I can do so without robbing myself of rest, however, I shall be glad to say a few words in the Temple. There is only one thing I consis-

---

*Stephen Samuel Wise (1874–1949), an American rabbi and scholar, helped found and was president of the Zionist Organization of America, the American Jewish Congress, the World Jewish Congress, and the Jewish Institute of Religion. He was perhaps the most influential American Jewish leader of the first half of the twentieth century.

tently refuse, and that is entertainment in the form of receptions or other hand-shaking functions. Also, I avoid dining in public before speaking.

You may pass on my letter whole, if you like. Writing all this to you was my way of making one letter do for two. You see I am doing my own drudgery of writing!

Sincerely yours,

56. To Thomas A. Watson [BP]

Scarsdale, N.Y.
September 17, 1915

My dear Mr. Watson:

You never saw me but that one time of my delightful visit to your home, under my husband's guidance, years ago, but as Amadeus Grabau's wife you will remember me I am sure.

In 1906 he borrowed of you one hundred and fifty dollars—I still recall the charmingly cordial note that accompanied your check—and while you have probably forgotten the matter, he has not; for as a debt that year after year he was obliged to leave outstanding the matter has worried him not a little. All these years—fourteen in all—he has been rendering his University distinguished service, building up his department to twenty times its capacity before he came, and making it a recognized center for research in his specialty, so that students come to him from every part of the world. His compensation for this high maximum of service has been a salary of twenty-five hundred dollars—his initial salary when he was called here as a lecturer; mechanical promotion to the rank of full professor, and a degree of personal recognition among his colleagues somewhat less than is accorded him in certain circles outside.

As an old friend, I thought you would be interested to know that the splendid work he has been doing, of which you may possibly have been aware through his numerous important publications, including a stupendous work on "The Principles of Stratigraphy," has been done on an uphill course, against the drag and discouragement of a very meager income and scant recognition. His big work looks to me twice as big when I look back on the years filled in the crannies, if not in the mass, with petty worries about household bills. You can imagine how glad I have been of the good fortune which in recent years has enabled me, through my writing, to relieve him somewhat of these harrowing things. In particular, it will give me great pleasure to present him with a receipt for the amount he has owed you all these years, when you will be so good as to acknowledge the enclosed check.

The amount, $232.70, I copied from a memorandum Amadeus made figuring the interest due. I don't understand compound interest, but I suppose Amadeus's figures are correct. He is to be surprised with the receipt so I could not safely discuss the matter with him in advance. I asked casually how much he owed you, and the answer was some scribbling which ended with the sum I take to be the amount due you at this time.

With many thanks for the help you have been to us, I am

Sincerely yours,

57. To Thomas A. Watson [BP]   Scarsdale, N.Y.
                                         September 25, 1915

My dear Mr. Watson:

I thank you for your letter of the 21st with too many enclosures. I shall present all the documents to Amadeus on an anniversary that occurs soon. I am sure he must accept the remittance of the interest in the spirit of friendship in which it was made, but I am bound to let him see that I *tried* to be businesslike.

The law of compensation has worked again. Had we not been too poor to pay our debts, I should have had no occasion to draw out your warmhearted comment on my book. I am happy to know that among those who have cared to learn how it feels to be made an American have been old friends of my husband's like you and Mrs. Watson.

With cordial greetings to your household, I am

Sincerely yours,

58. To Abraham Cronbach [AJA]   The Planters Hotel Co.
                                         St. Louis, U.S.A.
                                         November 10, 1915

My dear Rabbi Cronbach:

May I make you my messenger, to carry my thanks to the several members of your Temple family at whose homes I was so pleasantly cared for? As you know I shun, as a rule, private entertainment, but if I could be sure in advance of such gentle, considerate treatment at the hands of hosts and hostesses I should never again seek the harsh privacy of hotels.

Looking back upon that experience, I wonder how you all made it so restful for me, considering I inhabited two separate homes in that short visit!

To you, dear Dr. Cronbach, I owe much of the feeling I took away from South Bend of having spent my effort to some purpose. It is all very well to be received with enthusiasm, and applause is an agreeable accompaniment to one's speech, but oh! how one longs for some sign that something has been set in motion, besides a momentary response, by one's utmost effort! You who are of the exhorting brotherhood will know what I mean. I come into a strange place, I am met by many kind faces, sped on my way by many kind words and tokens—and there the little ferment ends, so far as I can see. "What will you *do* about it?" I always cry in my heart. It means so much, then, to see a definite attempt made to embody the fleeting messenger's hopes in some form of action. Your endeavor to place the books I referred to where the townspeople may get further acquainted with these matters—that in itself is a great deal. And I actually believe that South Bend will call upon me to keep my promise someday to come and see things *done,* not merely talked about, in the immigrant world of your city. I shall be entirely at your command when you have made a scientific survey of your immigrant population and coordinated your educational, civic and philanthropic agencies till it becomes difficult for an alien to remain an alien in your midst. Where there is so much will, there will be a way!

   With many thanks for a thousand self-sacrificing courtesies, I remain

                                                        Cordially yours,

59. To Ruth F. Woodsmall [SS]   2712 Webster St.
                                                   San Francisco
                                                   April 11, 1916

Miss Ruth F. Woodsmall
717 N. Tejon Street
Colorado Springs, Colo.

Dear Madam:

   Your letter of March 8th was a long time finding me, and I am afraid you may have given up expecting an answer by this time.

   I could not think of neglecting a communication like yours, written, as you assure me, in a kindly spirit of inquiry. Not a person that has ever had any experience on the lecture platform but knows that sometimes our utmost endeavor to make ourselves understood fails, and leaves a hundred questions in the minds of the audience which we would gladly answer if an opportunity were given us.

   You very rightly observe that an expression of gratitude for what America has done for the immigrant would be a fitting preface to any criticism of America's handling of the immigration problem. I am so entirely of your opinion on this point, that I have filled three hundred sixty-four printed pages with my acknowledgments of America's noble achievement in this field. I refer you to my story *The Promised Land,* a copy of which you will probably find in your local library. You will notice by the date of publication that my praise of America preceded by several years my criticism. If, after having made my cordial acknowledgments, I proceeded, like any other American, to study and think and criticize, it is only what you would expect of any of your fellow citizens who are eager to see that the full measure of virtue is extracted from our peculiar American institutions, for the good of all of us.

Referring to my talk in Colorado Springs, I am under the impression that I did briefly sum up, even on that occasion, my appreciation of what America has done for her adopted children, but I put the greatest emphasis on things America has not done, and that I did with a view to reminding the people of your town of what the country at large was getting ready to do by way of wiping out the many sins of omission, as well as certain acknowledged sins of commission, which have to be put in the balance along with the good that has been done to the immigrant, in order to arrive at a just estimate.

My plea for unrestricted immigration is based on what to many appears a fanatical doctrine, but I cannot take any other stand on the subject as long as American political and social principles loom bigger to me than any questions of expediency. May I refer you, for a more exact statement of my view on this branch of the immigration question, to my book *They Who Knock At Our Gates?* I am not in the habit of thrusting my writings under the notice of my correspondents, but in the two books to which I have referred, I have stated my position more accurately than I ever can do in an impromptu talk, and since you seem to be anxious to arrive at an understanding of my views, I have no choice but to tell you where you will find them stated.

As to my criticisms of the attitude of the American community towards the immigrant, and my recommendations of reforms, I must remind you that, as I stated in the course of my lecture, I am by no means alone in making these criticisms and demands. At the national conference on Americanization and Immigration at Philadelphia last January, several hundred delegates, representing every sort of institution, public and private, religious and secular, educational and civic, that had had anything to do with the immigrant, stood up one after another and clamored for a revision of our policy towards the immigrants already in our midst. The question of admission or restriction was dropped for the time being, but on the question of the treatment of the immigrant already with us there was an impressive unanimity of opinion: a change has got to come—and many specific recommendations were made as to what form the change shall take. If you care to follow up the matter, you can get information about this conference, and about the national Americanization work I referred to in my talk, by applying to the National Americanization Committee, 18 W. 34th Street, New York City.

For a brief resume of the grievances of the immigrant which are to be set against the acknowledged advantages, may I refer you to a statement by one who has for years devoted herself to the study of the immigration problem in all its phases—who is, like yourself and your friends, a descendent of the builders of our nation, and who cannot, like me, be suspected of being unduly prejudiced in favor of the immigrant. Look up the article "Lo, the Poor Immigrant" by Frances A. Kellor, in the *Atlantic Monthly* of January, 1916.

In closing, let me assure you that I appreciate the earnest and kindly spirit which prompted you and your friends to express your objections as you did. It is the indifference of a great part of the community that hurts the immigrant, as well as the rest of America, rather than inquiry and discussion like yours.

Very sincerely yours,

60. To Horace M. Kallen [AJA]

Scarsdale, N.Y.
August 11, 1916

Dr. Horace M. Kallen
University of Wisconsin
Madison, Wis.

My dear Dr. Kallen:

I was to let you know whether and when I could repeat my visit at Madison next season.

I am informed by my managers that between Appleton, Wis., on October 14th, to Alma, Michigan, on the 19th, I am to have a holiday. I haven't studied out the distances on the map, but I can see that I have a few days to spare, probably a longer interval than I am soon likely to have again.

I shall be delighted to put that time in in Madison, provided it is convenient for you.

If I remember aright, you will not be wanting me to speak on this occasion. It is just to be a neighborly, human visit; you to show me the University and country round about, and I to enjoy myself. Please do not understand me to be making any stipulations. If you want to put me to work, I will do whatever you wish. I only want you to know that I have a genuine desire to get acquainted with Madison, quite apart from any professional use that might be made of me.

I want to thank you for the inspiration I received at the Zionist Convention. I doubt if I should have thought of attending it, if it had not been for what you said to me at Madison.

Cordially yours,

61. To Horace M. Kallen [AJA]

National Hughes Alliance
Women's Committee
511 Fifth Avenue
New York, N.Y.
September 29, 1916

Dr. Horace M. Kallen
University of Wisconsin
Madison, Wis.

My dear Dr. Kallen:

I am very sorry that I have to forego my proposed inspirational holiday at Madison in the middle of October. I have been drafted for a piece of campaign work—Hughes, of course!—which obliges me to cancel all previous engagements in October. I do hope you will continue to keep your latch string out for me. Madison attracts me, particularly the possibility of being of some use to you there.

With best wishes for the New Year, which should be a great year for Zionism, I am,

Cordially yours,

62. To Horace M. Kallen [AJA]

Scarsdale, N.Y.
November 6, 1916

Dr. Horace N. Kallen
University of Wisconsin
Madison, Wis.

My dear Dr. Kallen:

I have not your recent letter at hand or I should enjoy answering it more to the point. It was such an amusing letter from a man of your way of thinking that it was too good to keep to myself. Accordingly I passed it on to Miss Kellor, to whom you also paid your compliments and in the confusion of life on the Campaign Train, the epistle has not been returned to me.

I thought you and I and Frances Kellor had approximately the same ideas on the subject of Americanism. How I did enjoy your article on that subject in the "Immigrants in America Review"! I still think that we are somewhere near the same camp on that subject, even if the shock of campaign differences seems to have established an abyss between us.

It was awfully amusing to find myself cast into "a harem of the intellect." This one of your picturesque phrases has stuck you see. You do not even pay us the compliment of assuming that we women have actual personal convictions on election questions. You make us out to be all blind followers of the beloved Colonel. Well, I do love him, for one, which does not prevent me from differing from him occasionally.

Let me tell you parenthetically that as far as the work of the Women's Train is concerned, we are not beaten even if we do lose the election. You will hear from us later.

Now let me fall back for comfort on the knowledge that we still have one great cause in common, namely Zionism.

I hope to make up for my postponed visit to Madison sometime during the season.

Sincerely yours,

63. To Horace M. Kallen [AJA]

Scarsdale, N.Y.
November 25, 1916

My dear Dr. Kallen:

The Players write me "You can make up your cancelled visit to Madison, Wis., during the week of Feb. 25th." They also tell me that the University of Wisconsin is trying to arrange for me to give "some lectures in the state." That's as near as I can tell when I'll hit your country.

You needn't spare me when I get there. I made my debut before the *Menorah* world at the University of Iowa a week ago.* It was an impromptu meeting, but we were all there, and glad to look on one another's faces.

There is much I feel like saying by way of comment on your further re-

---

Menorah Journal was published by the Intercollegiate Menorah Association in New York from 1915 to 1962.

marks about women in general, women in politics, and women followers of Hughes, but we'd never be done tossing that ball back and forth; and, besides, I'm just lazy enough, after my recent exertions, to sum up instead of expatiating. Briefly, then, you make me tired, Mr. Harry Kallen. I hope you'll atone by a steak supper—with salad—when I get to Wisconsin.

Sincerely yours,

64. To Horace M. Kallen [AJA]   Scarsdale, N.Y.
                                               November 29, 1916

Dear Dr. Kallen:

My managers have written me that the University of Wisconsin would like to have me fill twenty-one consecutive dates next summer, under the auspices of the Extension Division. The extension work of the western state universities excites my admiration. I still thrill over the idea of the university going to the people—I haven't got over that phase of my appreciation of things American, and never shall, I fear. I believe in the work, but lecture work in the summer is a fearful proposition, and I have always refused so far. I am writing my managers that I *may* risk it, after hearing the details of the program, provided (1) the University will pay a fee the size of a bribe and (2) I find I can use the occasion to advantage for the Zionist cause.

Will you give me your advice on three points:

1. Do you know the *summer* work in Wisconsin to be of sufficient importance to make it worth while?

2. Is the climate endurable?

3. Can anything of consequence be done in the Zionist field in the summer?

I shall be very grateful if you can help me out of your near acquaintance with the field.

Sincerely yours,

65. To Horace M. Kallen [AJA]   Scarsdale, N.Y.
                                               December 6, 1916

Dear Dr. Kallen:

Thank you for warning me off Wisconsin in summer. It relieves me of the necessity of being heroic.

It is good to know that you are coming to New York. If you are to have a strenuous time, it will do you good to come out to Scarsdale some evening. My sister will make you Hanukkah pancakes (לאטקעס, to be exact), and the children will dance for you. Don't you want to try us?

I hope you won't be too busy to let me know, in advance, your exact lecture dates in New York. I want to hear you and so does my sister.

Be careful about that February date. The Players said *about* Feb. 25th; I think I've had no more definite instructions.

Sincerely yours,

66. To Abraham Cronbach [AJA]

Scarsdale, N.Y.
December 13, 1916

Dear Mr. Cronbach:

You make me happy, and you will make the whole family happy.

We'll have the candles. Do bring the song books. There will be between fifteen and [or] twenty of us—I haven't heard from some of the friends invited—but you needn't burden yourself with twenty volumes. We can double up.

I did have an ambition that local shops do not permit me to realize, and perhaps you can help. I wanted to get hold of some of those real old fashioned slim wax tapers that we used to stick to the window casing Hanukkah nights—those of us in Polotzk who were too poor to have brass Menorahs or oil lamps. I've never seen these in this country, but I always meant to hunt for them.

We look forward especially to your part on our informal program.

Cordially yours,

Mary Antin with Josephine in 1908

CHAPTER FOUR

Illness and Gould Farm

1917–1936

The U.S. entry into World War I in 1917 signaled an end to Antin's productive, happy, and involved life. The downward spiral began as her husband, Amadeus Grabau, loyal to his German heritage, sided with Germany. Grabau's pro-German statements led to his dismissal from Columbia University in 1917 and ultimately to the breakup of the Antin-Grabau marriage. Their daughter, Josephine, recalls fierce political arguments raging daily until her parents, wanting to spare her the belligerent atmosphere, decided to separate.* During this time, whether as a result of the separation from Grabau or from a genetic illness lying dormant until that trauma, Antin began to suffer from mental illness. That the husband of one of America's foremost patriots supported the enemy must have caused her great shame and surely compounded her suffering.

Throughout 1917 Antin struggled in vain to maintain her lecture tour and her other interests. The absence of lecture fees and Grabau's income made money very scarce. Her financial state and emotional fragility necessitated the sale of the home in Scarsdale. With the aid of her brother, Harry, she sold the house and moved in with her sister Ida in Winchester, Massachusetts. She no longer spoke in public nor did she work on political campaigns. Soon she was to give up control of her money, living always with one of her sisters or in a sheltered living situation. Her mental health continued to decline, and by the early 1920s she was a patient at Austen Riggs Psychiatric Center in Stockbridge, Massachusetts.

We can only speculate about the origin and diagnosis of the mental ill-

---

*Josephine Grabau Ross, interview by editor, Averill Park, N.Y., Nov. 17, 1991.

ness that plagued Antin. It apparently began in 1916 or 1917, and although the term *neurasthenia* applied to symptoms now attributed to chronic fatigue syndrome or depression disappeared from medical usage as a diagnosis around 1910, an entry in the 1971 edition of *Notable American Women* states, "In 1918 Mary Antin suffered an attack of neurasthenia from which she never recovered."* Antin referred to it at different times as "a nervous breakdown," "a psycho-neurosis," and "a deep soul sickness." Although she was receiving care for mental illness in 1930 when the concept that one's nerve force has a limited and exhaustible energy supply was outmoded, she cited rest as her prescribed treatment. "My doctor does not wish me to write at present. He does not want me all stirred up," she reported to Agnes Gould.† Clara Antin, discussing her sister's past illness and wanting to make clear that Antin was not insane, said that her sister had "an emotional ill-health period."‡ Perhaps the most telling description of her illness comes from Harriet Phillips, Antin's friend at Gould Farm, who told me that her behavior was often manic, that she would commonly try to arrange dancing sessions before breakfast or that she would become very enthusiastic about numerous projects almost simultaneously, attempting to enlist the entire farm community in her plans.§ If this behavior was accompanied by periods of depression Antin may have suffered from what is now called bipolar disorder, the illness with which her daughter, Josephine, has been afflicted since her youth. More than thirty years would have to pass before sufferers of mental illness could find relief in psychotropic drugs. If Antin had lived in more recent times, she very possibly could have recovered her health and returned to her writing.

In 1923, Antin moved from Austen Riggs to the nearby Gould Farm in Monterey, Massachusetts. Gould Farm, at that time, was an alternative facility for mental-health patients. William Gould, a Protestant minister who believed the mentally ill could recover by living in a religious family setting and working productively on the farm, ran the complex with his wife, Agnes.

After Antin had been at the farm for a short time she became very attached to the Goulds, especially William (known at the farm as Brother

*Oppenheim 1991, 109; Handlin 1971.
†Antin to Gould, Feb. 23, 1930. Gould, wife of the farm's founder, was Antin's longtime friend.
‡Clara Antin, interview by Henry Laskowsky, Belmont, Vt., Oct. 1972, tape in my possession.
§Harriet Phillips, interview by editor, Monterey Mass., Nov. 9, 1991.

Will), and under his influence became interested in Christianity and a spiritual life. Initially, she considered him a Christ figure, following him, taking notes, and revering his every word. The nurturing atmosphere of the farm appealed to the emotionally bruised Antin, and she gave herself over to the caregivers and their religion.

The 1920s were lost years for Antin. She remained at Gould Farm, trying to piece together a meaningful existence. Her literary creativity disappeared, and bitterness set in with the realization that this was to be her life: a promising future unfulfilled as she became dependent on the generosity of others. A letter written in 1925 seemingly in response to a request for biographical information for a Houghton Mifflin publication prompted Antin to write, "As a contemporary I really don't exist."*

Acclimating to life at Gould Farm, she developed lifelong friendships with several of the residents: Agnes Gould, whom she had promised, after Brother Will's death, to write a history of the farm (a promise unfulfilled that caused Antin guilt that festered for years); Mildred Schlessinger, her friend and confidante; Caroline Goodyear, a resident and benefactor of Gould Farm, a relative of the Goodyear Tire Company's founder; Harriet Phillips, at this writing still a resident at Gould Farm; and Sydney and Rose McKee, whose son William made available to the author many of Antin's papers that were at the facility.

There followed a period of time when Antin lived a nomadic life, moving between Gould Farm, family members, and various hospitals. In 1930, back at the farm, she received an invitation from Thomas A. Watson, the "Mr. Watson" who as a young man worked with Alexander Graham Bell on the development of the telephone. Watson, by this time a successful industrialist, had been a friend of Antin and her husband when Grabau was at Columbia University. He invited Antin and her daughter to meet the mystic Meher Baba at a retreat at Harmon-on-Hudson in New York State.

Meher Baba, born in India in the late nineteenth century of Persian descent, declared himself an avatar when he was a young man and determined to live a life of silence, communicating by means of an alphabet board and hand gestures. Even today, many years after his death, Baba's disciples revere him, visiting the shrine at his birthplace and meeting throughout the year on Meher Baba property in Myrtle Beach, South Carolina.

*Antin to Dale Warren, Dec. 17, 1925. Warren was employed by Houghton Mifflin, probably in the publicity department.

Antin and her daughter soon became avid followers of Meher Baba. Despite her very independent nature, even as a young woman, Antin, paradoxically, exhibited some form of male hero-worship throughout her life. Her father was Antin's first hero. In *The Promised Land* she imbued him with lofty qualities when he brought his children to school for the first time. "[With] a voice full of feeling . . . he spoke of visions, like a man inspired. [He] was not like other aliens."* His standing as a Talmudic scholar was worthy of high praise in a letter to Israel Zangwill. Further, she had married at a relatively young age a highly educated professor eleven years her senior. She wrote that he was her "hero," that "he brought glory into [her] life." Later, at Gould Farm, Antin revered William Gould, who appeared to the lonely woman to have God-like qualities. And then followed the adoration of Meher Baba whom she accepted as an incarnation of God. Even in her late sixties she used the same sort of reverent language for Rudolph Steiner.†

For the next four years, until 1933, Antin and her daughter lived in Harmon-on-Hudson at Meher Baba's retreat. They were reluctant to return to Gould Farm and become involved in a farm project because the discipline of Baba's organization demanded an allegiance that might suddenly call them away on a moment's notice. Antin's passion for Baba surprised Watson, who had soon become disenchanted with the mystic. Although Antin also ultimately lost interest, all her descendants but one are still Baba followers and are completely separated from Jewish life. Jeanne Ross, Antin's great-granddaughter, recently married a Jew and is discovering her Jewish heritage.

By 1934 Antin seemed to have separated herself from the mysticism of Meher Baba (there is no further mention of him in her letters), but she continued to be absorbed by mysticism and the occult. Her return to Gould Farm, however, brought her back to a Christian setting where she believed these new subjects were not appreciated by her former friends. Still, she corresponded with others who shared her interest and in 1937 published "The Soundless Trumpet,"‡ an article dealing with the occult.

While at Gould Farm, Antin maintained an underlying attachment to mysticism and mystical writings. Out-of-body experiences, which she called "illuminations," fascinated her and became the subject of her let-

---

*Antin 1912a, 162.

†Rudolph Steiner (1861–1925), an Austrian social philosopher and writer, was a teacher of the spiritual doctrine of anthroposophy.

‡Antin 1937.

ters. She attempted to elicit the interest of the other residents, claiming some success by introducing the work of a writer of mystical tracts, Margaret Prescott Montague (1893–1955), and inviting her to the farm. As she would do later when a new hero, Rudolph Steiner, appeared, Antin attempted to proselytize among her friends.

Antin lived at Gould Farm as both patient and, later, as secretary and fund-raiser. It became her home and refuge, a place to which she would return many times. Rosemary Antin, her sister, lived there for a time after her own breakdown. Antin's daughter, Josephine, joined her there periodically, and much later Josephine Grabau Ross brought her daughters to the farm for summer vacations. Even now, the Antin granddaughters maintain ties with their grandmother's friends Harriet Phillips and Roma Foreman, longtime residents at Gould Farm.

67. To Horace M. Kallen [AJA]

Scarsdale, N.Y.
April 14, 1917

Dear Dr. Kallen:

The accompanying MSS are all I have been able to get out of Jessie. She has referred to others that are not in shape to be shown around. Without giving away the secret, I'm afraid I can't do any more now, as she is absorbed in some writing—she writes me this in a very tense mood—which she doesn't want to hold up for anything.

From her letters, I find that she thinks I am trying to place her poems in some magazine. I did once make such an effort, and she naturally got the idea that I'm at it again. Now she is very anxious to sell her things—will she ever forgive me for sharing this confidential bit?—so as to be able to go to the convention in Detroit; otherwise, she says, she must stay away. Now what?

If you still think the venture venturable, under present strained conditions, and *if* the volume circulates among Zionist friends, I suppose eventually the author would be nothing out by failure to connect with a magazine. But—Well, what do you say? Shall we steal the MSS and go ahead?

In this her first collection, there ought to be included the best of her pieces already published. Most of them appeared in the *Maccabaean*, some in the *Menorah*. I haven't the files accessible (I'm living nowhere in particular—have been down to the bottom, physically and every way, since I played around Madison) so I can't help you sift those out. I can't think who besides Jessie herself would have a complete file of her printed things. It would be a pity to omit any of her best things that may have appeared I don't know where. Certainly I'm of small use, where I thought I could help a lot.

To give you an inkling of Jessie's own rating of the poems I am forwarding, I am enclosing her recent letters about them; also some letters addressed to her by others. With fear and trembling I do this, lest in my clumsy judgment things seem communicable to a third person which Jessie would not want to pass beyond the personal. Jessie Sampter is one of the most delicate things I know. I'm a brute beside her, and I'm afraid to touch things that are near and personal to her. Please return the letters, and do see that no harm comes to Jessie from my meddling.

All the poems referred to in her two letters as accompanying them are included in the present packet.

68. To Horace M. Kallen [AJA]

Boston, Mass.
May 2, 1917

Dear Dr. Kallen:

Have you given it up? From your failure to prompt me I almost believe it.

I had laid aside my letter of Apr. 14, with Jessie's papers, to finish the next morning, from some notes I had made about the poems. I was taken ill, and other things happened, and I was where I didn't care what became of people and manuscripts and things. Now I'm picking up things again, and first thing I'm sending off your packet, hoping that, if your plans have not altered, my delay has not made the thing hopeless. It will be hard to learn that but for my failing you the thing might have gone through. However, there are heaps of hard things—and jolly ones. Aren't there, Sir Philosopher?

I can't make anything of my notes about the poems. They were jotted down for immediate use. You lose nothing, however, by my failure to express myself. My opinion wouldn't be any guide.

It would be a great pleasure, and a salve to my conscience as well, if I were permitted to read the proofs or perform any sort of drudgery in connection with the book, if a book there is to be.

Have you thought of getting Mitchell Kennerly on this thing?* He published some of Jessie's things before.

---

*Mitchell Kennerly (1878–1950) was the publisher of *Forum magazine*.

I am not dependable yet—have just added a sprained ankle to my more serious disabilities—but do give me a chance to make up, if there is occasion—

I was just thinking that swearing is a very noble exercise. What's your favorite swear?

Yours,

69. To Horace M. Kallen [AJA]

Scarsdale, N.Y.
May 17, 1917

Dear Dr. Kallen:

I have just received your letter about Jessie Sampter's poems, and have written to Miss Szold to get in touch with her. I'll do everything I can to hurry things along. I now have the advantage of being where everybody is—near New York. Do you know about Jessie's new book? Miss Szold had that MSS also in her hands.

Sincerely yours,

70. To Horace M. Kallen [AJA]

Scarsdale, N.Y.
May 23, 1917

Dear Dr. Kallen:

Miss Szold is writing you for both of us. We find ourselves in absolute agreement about the matter of giving Jessie's new work precedence over the collected poems, and about having Jessie's own judgment on anything published.

My letter to Miss Szold, stating my second thoughts, namely, that nothing should be put out without Jessie's knowledge, crossed one from her expressing the same view. I only wonder at myself that I put the matter so mildly, and so tardily. The folly of the idea of going without Jessie's judgment was obscured by the fine and just sentiment of the project as a whole. But we're all going to agree to take the safe way, aren't we? I couldn't have anything to do with the scheme otherwise.

The Book of the Nations, which Miss Szold is sending you, is surely the best thing Jessie has done, and a noble piece of work by any standards.* What you so justly say of the content of the earlier poems, that

---

*Jessie Sampter. 1917. *The Book of the Nations* (New York: Dutton).

it is not novel, applies also to the new poem. The distinction of all Jessie's things seems to me to lie in their feeling. The new poem resembles the Bible in more than form. Let us see what we can do with it.

Sincerely yours,

71. To Bernard G. Richards [JT]   Winchester, Mass.
June 12, 1918

Mr. Bernhard G. Richards
1 Madison Avenue
New York, N.Y.

My dear Mr. Richards:

In answer to your letter of May 13th I am sorry to say that I have no plans for being in New York for a long, long time. I am recuperating, in a tent, from a recent breakdown. If you travel as far afield as Boston, you will find me at Winchester, only six miles from the heart of the town, where I shall be delighted to discuss the project to which you refer.

Sincerely yours,

72. To Horace M. Kallen [AJA]   Winchester, Mass.
October 9, 1918

Dear Dr. Kallen:

Why in the world haven't you written a review of Jessie Sampter's "Book of the Nations"? I happen to know that you think well of it, and I'm sure you want to see it circulate outside the borders of the Zionist community. It hasn't been presented to the bigger world with anything like the emphasis it deserves. I don't know why it isn't up to you as much as to anybody.

You can't turn on me with the same challenge, because you know I don't know how to do a review. When are *you* going to do it?

Sincerely yours,

Perhaps I ought to explain this sudden onslaught. The explanation is simple. I am just emerging after a long period of retirement—and blessed *silence!*—due to illness. Picking up loose ends is my principal occupation at present.

73. To Horace M. Kallen [AJA]   Winchester, Mass.
                                                      October 20, 1918

Dear Dr. Kallen:

We are near neighbors, as long as you remain in Roxbury. Call up Winchester 144 and say when you feel like a walk in the country, or, what is more like me these days, a talk in the sunny quiet where my tent still stands. The tent must be folded away presently. Come very soon and would you bring your sister?

We have no street number, and are rather hard to find. My sister will tell you how to do it, when you telephone. It's her special art, getting people up our hill the direct way. We may meet you where you leave the car, if you'll say when.

Then we'll talk about Miss Sampter and other folks.

                                                      Cordially yours,

74. To Thomas A. Watson [BP]   Winchester, Mass.
                                                      September 11, 1920

Dear Mr. Watson:

Thank you for letting me see the correspondence between yourself, Prof. Crosby and Amadeus.* No man ever had truer friends than Amadeus has in you two.

It was hardly proper for A. to quote me in support of his request for a loan. As you know, my knowledge of his affairs has been derived from the reports you were good enough to send me from time to time, and from what Josephine had to say after her occasional visits to him. These fragments, however, amounted to a pretty full understanding of his circumstances when pieced out of my knowledge of his ways and habits in the past. In addition, there were the occasional revealing glimpses I had of him when I was obliged to escort Josephine as far as his doorstep, the last time being in June.

When you sent me news of his appointment, a great burden was lifted from my heart. The picture of his miseries, both physical and social, has never ceased to oppress me. I was glad for him as nobody else could possibly be, not even you two loyal friends who are standing by him in this

---

*Professor Crosby taught in the Paleontology Department at Columbia University with Amadeus Grabau and, according to Clara Antin, was dismissed at the same time.

critical moment. But, I had many fears and uncertainties about his ability to carry off the project. There was some notion in my mind that he might owe his appointment in part to his Chinese students of some years back, who knew him at Columbia at his best. Would they find him changed for the worse? Would they be disappointed? He used to be presentable socially, and so winning. Will these qualities bloom again with professional and social rehabilitation?

Anxieties about big things and about things in themselves little, but big in their effects, flocked around his image. When I saw him in June he was a shocking figure: not only shabby in the extreme, but apparently confirmed in shabbiness and not over scrupulously clean. I dared not think what he was like beneath the exterior. His teeth were black with neglect—really black. It used to be a day's work to get him off to the dentists, and now of course, he had had the best excuses for not frequenting the dentist for a long time.

These sorry externals added to his painfully diseased appearance made of him a figure that did not fit into the picture of a man taking charge of a laborious and important enterprise under the direct auspices of a great government.

I wrote him a very urgent letter, with my congratulations on his good fortune, recommending as tactfully as one could in my anxious position, two things: that he make an earnest effort to prove to himself whether Dr. Turck could start him on a cure, to be continued in China (you know about Dr. Turck and his cure of a similar case); and that he take care to fit himself out properly in the matter of clothes. I knew from you that he was borrowing money to get away; I knew much more than you, though I had not one single word direct from him. I knew he would be enormously in debt and would make an effort to pay all his petty debts at least before leaving the country. I don't remember what I said about a thousand dollars; probably that he ought to fit himself out presentably even if he had to incur so large a debt as that size—in which I was allowing two or three hundred dollars for clothing, which would be only a modest allowance at present prices. I doubt if he has a decent article of underwear at this minute, and his dentist's bill would run up to a couple of hundred more.

Prof. Crosby asks what is Amadeus to me or I to him. A woman would not need to ask that question. Amadeus is the man for whom I laid out clean linen as he needed it for fifteen years. Perhaps a man cannot understand that by the performance of these small personal services a woman fetters herself with a sense of responsibility that outlasts less material bonds. I am not a domestic woman; I have incurred enough reproach on that score to be quite convinced of it. Yet in all these dreary years since my exile from Scarsdale, when loneliness has oppressed me and emptiness of my heart sapped my very life, it would have been an unspeakable solace if I could have gone unseen secretly to him, to the place where he was, to put his rooms in order, mend his socks and dust his books.

Dear Mr. Watson:

Will you tell me if there is any legal way in which I may waive, in behalf of myself and Josephine, all claim to Amadeus's estate in favor of his creditors? If an informal statement is of any value, I hereby undertake to turn over everything he dies possessed of to his creditors if I have any authority over his estate at the time. I should like also to register a promise to use my own means to pay his debts if necessary; but to make such a promise in my present financial condition would be a piece of empty heroics I am not capable of.

I know well that both you and Prof. Crosby are ready to take the full risk of financing Amadeus's venture. It is not for your sakes that I want to cover the point of A's security, but in case he should be making application for further loans elsewhere. Will you instruct me how I may do this? You probably know enough law to save me a lawyer's fee in this matter. If not, will you tell me what lawyer I can go to? I don't know anybody except Mr. Jenner and I once told you how unsatisfactory I found a friend-lawyer to be. I am also barred from Mr. Jenner's services by his persistent refusal to accept any fee from me.

What is Amadeus to me? (I am not misunderstanding Prof. Crosby.) His query was not meant for my eye and in any case it was just a short-hand way of enquiring how matters stood between us. I understand, but still the question reaches down to something very deep in me, a protest, irrationally enough, against the implications that there might be—more than one answer to the question? I do not know what I am to Amadeus at this moment. He to me is the man who brought glory into my life and chaos. He is the one who cherished me like father and mother and lover and dearest friend in one. He is the one who wounded me and trampled on me and made sport of the sufferings he inflicted. Having him, I had heaven and earth for my own; losing him I have had to fight to be content with a broken life. He typified to me at one time my country's basic law; at another time, the canker growing on her vitals. In his eyes, I have seen honor, manhood, chivalry; also treason, cowardice, and bestiality. I have been nourished on his self-sacrifice, and mangled by his brutality. Because of him I have been all things, and less than nothing. What is Amadeus to me? I should have to take the enquirer once through heaven and once through hell to find images to symbolize what Amadeus stands for in my life.

But I am ashamed of letting myself go like this. The question is already answered, anyway, when I remind the enquirer that for 15 years I was responsible for Amadeus's clean linen. And you will forgive my outbreak.

I hope to tell you good news soon about Josephine. The final report from Trudeau should be here any day, and I am sure that the first favorable report will be sustained. What a world of trouble we have been through, from June to September, on account of a physician's error! But thank God this particular nightmare is dissolved into thin air.

Josephine certainly profited by Dr. Overton's unbased alarm. She has gained in weight (though her gain in height has almost neutralized that) and she was happy every day of the nine weeks at camp. She was awarded the highest honor there, the prize for "best camp spirit."

There was something I wanted to report about Josephine's attitude toward Amadeus, but I have written enough for once. I am tired and you will be.

Shall I see you in Boston?

Always yours,

75. To Thomas A. Watson [BP]
41 Granville St.
Dorchester, Mass.
December 4, 1920

Mr. Thomas A. Watson
67 Mount Vernon Street
Boston, Mass.

My dear Mr. Watson:

This is to confirm our several conversations in which you were good enough to accept the responsibility of disposing of my literary remains in the event of my death.

You will please take charge of all my manuscripts and dispose of them according to instructions which I have given you, or may give you from time to time. Everything for which you have no instructions to the contrary you will please destroy. I do not want any writing of mine to go to press without my final revision. I feel sure that the world will survive the loss of my unpublished works, if any, but I would hardly be able to rest in peace if any doubtful work of mine were published after my death.

Any manuscripts which are not covered by the foregoing instructions, I authorize you to dispose of according to your own best judgment. You will please submit them to one or other of the publishers whom we have sometimes discussed in connection with some of my papers, and make whatever arrangements you can for their publication.

The only considerable manuscript at this moment is the bulky one, the greater part of which is in your keeping, awaiting my revision. I intend to deposit copies of subsequent papers also with you, with instructions to cover them.

76. To Thomas A. Watson [BP]   Gould Farm
"Inwood," New Marlboro, Mass.
October 2, 1924

Dear Mr. Watson:

I have thought of you a great deal recently during my readings. I have just reread Carpenter's *Drama of Life [Love] and Death,* and I am astonished to realize how much more I am able to get from this writer than a few years ago.* I thought this would interest you as evidence that my education in mysticism has advanced very rapidly since I began this new life at Gould Farm. The bulk of my reading is in the general field of religion, mainly of the mystical order. I am learning a new language. My tendency, as you know, was always in this direction, but whereas formerly I nibbled feebly at this particular form of the bread of life, at this period I find myself able to derive from it most of my material for growth.

Let me tell you more about this when you come. Also, you will be amazed and pleased to learn what a tremendous increase of power, both physical and mental, I have received. I can hardly believe sometimes when at night I review the day just passed that I have expended so much energy and yet been left undepleted. Truly I am going from strength to strength under the grilling discipline of this life.

I am taking this time out of a very busy morning to touch on these matters, although you will be here soon, when we can talk, because now and then there comes over me the realization that I do so very little to make you aware of my tremendous prosperity of every form. You who were such a constant agonized witness of my days of tribulation, I do long to have you realize constantly and abundantly how completely you were justified in your unshakable faith through those dreary years when you were almost the only friend who, in full knowledge of my condition, never

*Edward Carpenter. 1912. *Drama of Love and Death* (New York: Mitchell Kennerly).

gave up hope of me. To you and Elizabeth I owe a world of love and gratitude for your faithfulness in the past.

I study the subject of Geulah in the new light, and still find it a profound and precious instruction.* I pray heartily for a conviction of sin in this respect—that, if there was indeed, sin, I might have the benefit of repentance. But I have had no answer to that prayer so far. I suspect I shall not be allowed any light on this question until I confess that whole chapter to some one with whom it might make a difference—the Goulds, perhaps? But I have to have your leave first, don't [I]? At any rate, I am in no degree troubled by the thought of the [illegible]. It is just one more subject for study.

77. To Mary Austin† [HH]

Gould Farm
Great Barrington, Mass.
March 11, 1925

Dear Mary Austin:

It is almost like talking to myself to write to you, because I have so long taken you into my inmost confidence, referring my great problems to you, inwardly; especially my professional problems on their spiritual side.

I am going to ask you presently what is the matter with me, and how to remedy what's wrong; actually address you by word, this time, instead of mentally asking myself what would Mary Austin think. I will omit the usual apologies for adding to your burden of unsolicited correspondence—don't I know what it's like!—I will only apologize for not using a typewriter. There's a reason!

I don't know the bulk of your writing, but I know you extremely well from the little I have read. I first knew you for a sister spirit (I know you will not repudiate the claim!) through your stories of the desert, and your interpretations of the Indian made me kiss your hands in loving gratitude. Stray articles of yours on Jesus, on the spiritual roots of artistic technique, placed you high up in the rank of my personal teachers. This last stage occurred when I had come to live, as I am now living, far from any library,

---

Geulah is a Hebrew word meaning redemption.

†Mary Hunter Austin (1868–1934) was an author of many works of fiction and nonfiction. Antin began to write to Austin after a mixup in their names led to a check belonging to Austin to be mailed to Antin. Antin was especially influenced by Austin's writing about mystical experiences that made Austin believe that there was a particular pattern to her existence influenced by the Cosmos.

or I would have hunted out everything you have written on these subjects. I shall do so the next time I am in a library, unless in the meantime
you will refer me to your best things, which I can order from a bookseller.
The present personal enquiry has to go just the same. I am impatient for
the application of your wisdom to my individual problem.

I hope you have read *The Promised Land,* which would be my introduction to you. I am going on from that, as if I knew you had read it.
That's a good piece of work, with all its obvious faults, and the best thing
about it, in my opinion, is that it says that the person who did it ought to
be able to do really fine things, after sufficient maturation and training.
The only things I have done are: an amazing mixture of naivete and rhap-
sody published under the title of *They Who Knock at Our Gates* ("they"
being the immigrants) and a few short stories, three of which were published (*Atlantic Monthly*), stories of which I was once enamored, which I
still think well of, and which, like my autobiography, promise better
things to come.

The better things haven't come. Nothing has come since 1914. The little I have published came out between 1911 and 1914. In 1914, the War.
My husband, a man of great genius in scientific research, a palaeontologist
of international reputation, who had initiated me into the meaning of love
and flawless marriage, suffered the peculiar moral cataclysm of German-
Americans, he being born on American soil of the German spirit. Because
I was spoiled and undisciplined I didn't know how to meet my catastro-
phe. The story of how my beautiful home was broken up, in spite of years
of spiritually clumsy though absolutely sincere efforts on my part to save
us all, is well indicated by an anonymous article, "Wives of German Americans," which appeared in the *Atlantic* during the interval before 1917
(?); an article which I might have written of my own household.*

In 1913 I found myself, through a series of curious accidents, launched
on a lecturer's career. To my amazement, for everything, I thought, was
against it, I had a great success. Driven by a sense of civic duty, I kept on,
although I hated the life and discounted the value of my efforts; and my
husband followed my public career with the same affectionate pride—a
pride almost paternal in its intensity—just as he had watched my literary
beginnings. It was he who collected volumes of newspaper clippings
about me and my doings.

When, in 1914, my lover-husband turned into a dreadful hostile
stranger who terrorized the household and scandalized the community

---

*M. L. S. 1918. "Wives of German Americans," *Atlantic Monthly* (June 17).

(no, I am not exaggerating; these are matters of history) I suffered, through my failure to adjust myself, a nervous break-down. Now commenced my real education, through the discipline of mind and heart in *nine years* of nervous derangement. I kept on with my lecture work, intensively till about 1916, sporadically for some time after that—during 1917–18 under war-time organizations. When I wasn't lecturing I was under treatment by an assortment of neurologists. I wasn't writing at all, not trying to. It wasn't till the summer of 1920 that I made the terrifying discovery that the reason I wasn't writing was not, as I had supposed, because I was fully engaged otherwise—lecturing, organizing and caring for three separate families broken and mutilated by the war, and always, always watching over my only child, a very gifted girl; studying and improvising to protect her from the shocks of the poor transfigured father and the disrupted home life. The reason I wasn't writing, I tardily discovered, was because I had lost the power to write.

A psychoneurosis, of course. My education continued, in the hells of sanitariums, at the hands of doctors of various schools of psychotherapy. At length, at the end of 1923, when I had been beaten to a pulp spiritually, I abandoned the doctors and entered on the life of prayer.

Immediately I was lifted up out of the pit. The miracle took place within a few days after my coming to Gould Farm (which is now my home), where for twelve years Mr. and Mrs. Gould have been reclaiming broken lives by the power of love and prayer. Their work has won the admiration of the leading psychotherapists, who send to Gould Farm all the cases that baffle their science; and Gould Farm takes them in as fast as room can be found for them. The technique of the Gould Farm "cures," the simplicity-in-profundity of Mr. Gould's processes—his original adaptations and unqualified applications of the teachings of Jesus, his amazing versatility, his challenging revolutionary economics—all this has become a profound study to me; and the burden has been laid on me, if I am not mistaken, to interpret the Goulds to the world, or to attract to Gould Farm a worthier interpreter, someone like Mary Austin.

Indeed I have thought of you in this connection more than once, you with your spiritual insight and your literary ease. But this letter is not to invite you, unless the little I have revealed of Gould Farm in itself invites you. I have set myself the task of challenging the attention of such as you, in a preliminary account of the farm, which I had expected to produce about this time. A year after I came here—last November to be exact—I suddenly felt the stirring of the writing part of me. All the year I had been completely contented, profoundly at peace, serving my apprenticeship in the humble service of love, after the Gould pattern, in kitchen and pantry and chamber—in whatever manual work I could lay my hand on—while at the same time assisting with the direct handling of patients, for which my own experience of invalidism and the resultant practical training in psychotherapy had somewhat fitted me. Washing pots or initiating patients—I prospered in everything. And I became skilled in extemporizing hymns of thanksgiving for the extraordinary increase of power I felt in every direction—physical, mental, spiritual. It was a genuine rebirth I had undergone, and He who had so miraculously healed me continued to instruct me. Vista after vista of the spiritual life opened to me, through my daily labor and study and reflection.

Then, all in that quietness which I had learned to regard as the best guarantee of authenticity, came the prompting to write. It was simply that a door had opened and I stood in another room. Mr. Gould had the same prompting concerning my writer's work at the same time. It is a frequent "coincidence" between us two, that the same inspiration hits us at the same moment. The Goulds knew—everybody knew—that I was carrying on a minute study of the life on the Farm all the time. My notebook is a pet family joke. And now everything was done to enable me to organize my day in such a manner that I might be at my writing.

There are cumulative indications that the next development of the Goulds' work must be in the directions of duplication—doing likewise elsewhere—and public interpretation. No one has come so far to interpret except myself. If I am sure of one gift that I have it is a trick for showing the hidden meaning of obvious things. Oral interpretations I am doing all the time. I now feel the urgency of literary interpretation—some preliminary articles, stories, by and by, if I grow sufficiently in power, [of] a life of W. J. Gould.

But I am having extraordinary difficulty. Where all other forms of disability have vanished, the writing faculty is still crippled. Of course that is, in a sense, the critical point: can I say I am restored if I cannot write with at least my old ease? I always was a slow, fumbling artisan with the pen, my output always extremely slim. I never had any technical training; I still doubt if such training is my primary need. I always knew that I wasn't a writer, but a channel for written words. In the old days I didn't know enough to ask the Great Teacher's help. Now I pray constantly to be used as a Channel of good tidings, a transmitter of beauty. I take my literary difficulties daily to my Father; as frequently indeed, as I become aware of them. I pray in particular to have my day's work laid out for me, to be shown if I am in error as to the call to write. I am entirely free from anxiety about the outcome—that I ought to put down in capitals, for it marks the difference between my present state and my past. My temptation is to take the line that I was mistaken as to the vocation—that it is not yet time to be writing. I so love the direct work with the patients, I love the healthy bustle of the kitchen, I love meeting the daily emergencies, the frequent call to a renewal of physical strength and mental elasticity without taking rest—I love and rejoice in the full impact of the wholesome strenuousness of this life. And I have developed a good deal of skill in it—I was counted on, while I was involved in the machinery, as I call it, as one of the principal workers. The solitary task of writing, in its present unfruitful state, does not yield any such satisfaction as the other. You see my temptation: there is no question of my usefulness in the more active work, while the other is one continued wrestling with ghostly shapes, in the expectation of some future usefulness. But I am held to my solitary task with its deferred satisfactions. Held. My prayers bring no indication that my "call" was an illusion, and I continue free from anxiety. I laugh at myself a good deal— a good sign, isn't it?—and I continue to let people think that I am about to bring forth the word that will be as a beacon lighting enquirers to Gould Farm, the materialization of the teachings of Jesus in the life of a community.

What can you tell me, Mary Austin? An instinct which I dare not disregard warns me not to reveal my difficulties to anyone here, not even to Brother Will (that's Will Gould). Brother Will must come in by and by; not at this stage. *You* can help. What must I tell you about my daily life, about my habits of praying and of writing, to enable you to make a diagnosis? I suppose that my primary failure is in the realm of prayer. What can you say?

If you are a reasonable journey away from here, perhaps you will come after all, to see Gould Farm for yourself. This, indeed, may turn out to be another instance of God moving in a mysterious way his wonders to perform. He gave me the writing faculty, I mislaid it, He prompts me to ask help of a finer artist than myself—and my task is accomplished in my finding an interpreter equal to the thing to be interpreted. Perhaps I should make it clear that while my conviction of the need of interpretation has been constant, the sense of myself as the interpreter has been less constant. Always there is the thought of the alternative, that not by my mouth but by the mouth of a messenger whom I should bring here shall the meaning of Gould Farm be published. That doubt as to my importance is characteristic, however. I always saw people who could do what I was doing far better, even when the public put me at the head of the column.

I always knew that my greatest successes were accidental; that I never achieved much by my conscious efforts, that things sometimes *got themselves done* through me. (Once, while facing an immense audience, I couldn't keep back the cry, "Why am *I* chosen, instead of any of these?")

I have read over what I have written. It is quite legible, so I don't hesitate to send it. It occurs to me, however, to write to your publishers first, to locate you, before sending on this weighty document. One isn't always stationed at the address given in *Who's Who!*

Two other points I want to touch on. (1) I am not a Christian—not in any technical sense of adherence to orthodox Christian dogma; not in any popular sense. One friend defines me as "a Christian *and* a Jew," making a distinction from the popular rather distasteful conception of a "Hebrew-Christian." I don't care what I am called, but I want to be sure I don't mislead anyone.

(2) Gould Farm is not the only subject that stirs my literary faculty. Old literary projects of such vitality that they have survived the years of the valley of the shadow, are now reviving. My stories that I didn't write, a novel—or is it a play?!—on the theme of unwelcome apotheosis. Yes, *plays.* I have to write plays. There is hidden in me the germ of more than one stirring photodrama—one on the life of John Woolman! And poems. Why is it I don't make poems? I *think* poems enough.

You see: I don't seem to be dead. Will you help me learn how to be more effectively alive?

Your disciple from afar,

78. To Bernard G. Richards [JT]   Gould Farm
                                                                                    Great Barrington, Mass.
                                                                                    June 2, 1925

Mr. Bernard G. Richards
414 Madison Avenue
New York, N.Y.

Dear Mr. Richards:

The book *In a Strange Land* reached me some time ago but I have not had time to look at it. I shall do so at the earliest opportunity, just out of interest in what you are publishing; but from an expression of opinion you will have to excuse me. It has been my rule, a rule forced on me by my profound conviction that I don't do that sort of thing at all well, not to express myself publicly about books.

I rather expect to be in New York next winter when I should indeed hope for an opportunity to renew acquaintance and hear of things Palestinian and others.

Sincerely yours,

79. To Thomas A. Watson [BP]   Gould Farm
                                        Great Barrington, Mass.
                                        September 14, 1925

Dear Mr. Watson:

I have just been looking over my will and the various documents, copies of which, with a copy of the will, I have deposited with you. I am going to alter my will slightly, as I consider the FOURTH item entirely out of harmony with the present situation. I intend to take care of this little business very soon after getting to New York, and then will send you a copy of the revised will.

Perhaps you have forgotten that you have undertaken the burden of literary custodianship. As everything has been left in the last analysis to your own judgment, perhaps no additional word from me is necessary. Nevertheless it has occurred to me to state explicitly that Mrs. Gould and other members of the Gould Farm family will be very glad to share with you the burden of deciding how to treat whatever of the Gould biography material I may leave unfinished. My feeling is that the notes which I have accumulated up to date could hardly be used by anyone else. I expect to work on this material all the coming winter, and will try to have the stuff in as usable a shape as possible. But I do hope that what I said to Mrs. Gould recently in [a] light mood will be taken seriously: namely, that none of you will permit yourself any heartbreaks if it turns out that this slow piece of work is left unfinished. I don't think any of us have a right to set our hearts on the completion or success of this writing. It is a great undertaking for a person with my particular limitations. I have worked as diligently at it, and shall continue to do so, as it is in me to work. For the outcome we have no guarantees. If I should drop out before this thing is in such shape that another can put it through, I shall be well pleased if your judgment permits you to clean out my filing cabinet and make a handsome bonfire of the contents.

It would be a substantial help to me to have an opportunity before long to go over this matter of the Gould biography with you. At this moment my literary custodian is less informed than anyone of half a dozen people with whom I have been discussing the subject. My realization of my job has matured greatly since last I saw you, and the progress I have made in assembling the material and approaching actual writing makes me very desirous of putting you in touch with the thing as a whole. May I hope to see you in New York before long?

80. To Dale Warren [BP]
Gould Farm
Great Barrington, Mass.
December 17, 1926

Mr. Dale Warren
Houghton Mifflin Co.
2 Park Street
Boston, Mass.

My dear Mr. Warren:

I suppose you are the publicity department, and that's why I never knew you. I was always short on the publicity dope, as Mr. Greenslett and others of the family will tell you.

And I am still deficient in that line. What must I do about the *Boston Herald* portrait gallery? It will soon be time for them to reheat that patriotic hash from *The Promised Land* which they have served up at shortish intervals, about Washington's Birthday, ever since Houghton Mifflin has been paying me royalties. Hadn't they better save me up for that?

If it has to be a "portrait," you'll have to find an old one, won't you? Anything less than ten years back would be anachronistic. Tuskegee Institute, Division of Photography (Tuskegee, Ala.) has a fairly recent picture, but it doesn't go with any legend you might pin to it, as the tale of my honorable performances breaks off long before the date of this photo. Unless this is a series of *contemporary* New Englanders why don't you use a nice blurb with a nice picture from 'way back? As a contemporary I really don't exist, you know; not as a celebrity. You might do a nice obituary, and perhaps I can help you with that.

Why, that's the line, surely. Something like this:

M—— A—— author of (*blaa, blaa, blaa*—where you tell them what a wonderful book *The Promised Land* is—started a deluge of immigrant autobiographies etc.—affected legislation etc.—translated etc.) and of (more *blaa, blaa* about *The Knockers*—that unique document in defense of Americanism at any cost—compared by a reviewer to old Amos—repented of by the author—etc.) Seldom has an author created so much of a flurry by such a meager literary performance. Just the two volumes named, and a very few short stories (*blaa, blaa*—ask Mr. Sedgwick) lost in what are now back numbers of the *Atlantic Monthly*. It is about ten years now since her last published story. What has happened to choke the (*blaa,*

blaa) literary gift which in the course of a few years' activity won the hearts of such a large reading public? (Statistics of sales etc.) M—— A—— dropped out of sight during the dark days of the war and has not been heard of since. A nervous breakdown is understood to have accounted for the greater part of this hiatus: but since her recovery? For her friends say that she came out of her valley of shadows in better health than she ever knew before in her life. Still her many admirers *(blaa, blaa)* wait in vain for a sign. One asks, what fatal crippling may have occurred in the process of nervous breakdown? One recalls the theory advanced by some observers of her meteoric career that her genius was seduced in its infancy, and hurt beyond repair, by the exploitation of the lecture platform. Coaxed into public work against her own conviction, by importunate appeals of great public leaders like Theodore Roosevelt and Jane Addams, she was an instant success on the platform *(blaa, blaa*—pages of slush on file at office of The Players, Boston, my managers), won her way with every type of audience, from grammar school assemblies to university forums—churches, prisons, political mass meetings (where her candidates were invariably defeated), national conventions of educators etc. etc. (statistics—from The Players). Opposed to those who saw danger for her in public life, there were many who valued M—— A——'s contribution as a publicist no less than her literary achievement. But over both phases of her activity suddenly fell the veil of obscurity, and no one can be found sufficiently informed, or sufficiently prophetic, to read us the riddle of M—— A——'s ten years' silence. *Who's Who* gives her address as Gould Farm, in the Berkshires. Shall we hear some day from Gould Farm, or will M—— A——'s career be likened finally to a skyrocket? That, as Hamlet would say, is the question. How's that? Cut to the right measure, of course. You will understand from the above that I was at least willing to help.

Sincerely yours,

81. To Mildred Schlessinger* [GF]

Very temporarily at
2875 Sedgwick Ave.
Bronx, N.Y.
January 6, 1928

You dear Mildred—dear, loving, faithful Mildred!

That is faithfulness in friendship, to keep on writing to the friend who owes you answer to five or six letters. Joking aside, it is lovely to count you

---

*Mildred Schlessinger was a resident at Gould Farm and Antin's friend.

among the friends who will never give me up, no matter what the outward signs are. But I haven't left anything like "five or six letters" of yours unanswered. Only two, counting this one of December 26. You know how systematic I am. I never file away a letter till it has been in some way attended to, and I find only one other letter of yours in my folder of unanswered letters. (Alas, there is always a goodly sheaf of them.) Not that I need mechanical aids to remind me of your letters that have not been answered: your every message leaves an impression on me, and I can tell without consulting my file any time at all whether I owe Mildred Schlessinger a letter. I quoted the file only as evidence. Undoubtedly I have lost some of your letters on account of many changes of address. I have lived in at least six different places during the past eleven months and vibrated between some of them so as to cause many more than six changes all together. I have been away from the Farm a great deal of this interval, partly on account of urgent family matters, partly in connection with some special studies and enquiries growing out of the biography-still-in-preparation. For example, I have been engaged in a study of the principles at work in what we call "religious healing," such as found at Gould Farm and elsewhere. *What* precisely helped Mildred Schlessinger, for instance, and *how* did it help her? Perhaps you can give me the answer yourself in your own simple transparent way; but a philosopher is bound to complicate every issue on the way to simplifying it, and that's me, I suppose! I wish I had a chance to tell you something of the things I am learning in the course of these enquiries.

I never fail to be touched, no matter how often I hear it, when I learn that you still remember me in your prayers. God bless you and bless you for faithfulness in prayer, perhaps the greatest faithfulness there is.

Dear girl, you must, you must get back to the Farm some time. You sound so wistful in your remembering of your one Christmas with us there. Five years ago, think of it. But it is very gratifying to find the picture of that time so fresh and clear in your heart after all these many Christmases. There is a precious tribute in your simple sincere word about the Farm: "All I know is that it is home."

It is fine to start the new year with the news that you are so steadily holding your gains. God bless Dr. Cobb and all workers in his field. Isn't the world just crowded with devoted people who live to help you and me?

What shall we read? To think of your having to go so far for suggestions! I am especially glad of your continued quest for worthwhile books, and happy to pass on to you a simple hint that will keep you busy with good reading for the rest of your life, if you wish. Ask at your branch library, or at the main library—the branch should serve you, if you make it a point—for some of the American Library Association leaflets "Reading with a Purpose." To read right straight through the courses there outlined is to acquire a university education. I haven't the list with me, as I am roaming around for a while, but I remember one or two courses that I would recommend as an introduction. "Pivotal Figures of History" is one and "Religion in Everyday Life" another (I may not give the titles exactly, but near enough to identify them, I think) and "The Life of Christ" another (that is the subject, if not the exact title, and you have already read, to my knowledge, at least one of the six books in the course on Christ. I put this course in specially because I remember your asking for books on this subject). I should start with the "Pivotal Figures," as there you have in the most illuminating form of biography a condensed view of world history, as a background for all other subjects.

Do let me know how your librarian treats you about "reading with a purpose," also what you are reading, from time to time. Write "Five or six" more letters, and I will try to reply to most of them! I feel as if I am myself starting on a wonderful adventure in starting you on these well-selected, varied, and interesting readings.

Here's all my love to you, and my thanks for your dear good letters. I am ever in your debt.

82. To Caroline Goodyear* [GF]   Chappaqua, N.Y.
                                           July 23, 1928

Dear Caroline:

You or Agnes or both of you must help me about Priscilla.† I lay awake, after saying goodnight to you two in your room on Friday night, fairly wriggling in embarrassment. How could I have been so stupid!—Priscilla Scovill, one of the wealthy members of the community, invited to hear my hard-luck tales! Why didn't I remember?! That was an awful break if ever there was one. It's my innocence that betrayed me—that, and my longing, growing stronger and stronger every time I'm around her, to keep her close in the things that matter to me. It was I who first dragged

---

*Caroline Goodyear (1868–1962), Agnes Gould's sister and a founder of Gould Farm, was one of the original associates.

†Florence Scovill, known as Miss Priscilla, was an English teacher at Erasmus High School in Brooklyn. She built a house at Gould Farm for the Goulds to live in and, after her retirement, moved to the farm herself.

her into Sally-conferences—I remember her insisting the first time that she wouldn't be of any use—and some time back I began to pour out my heart to her about Jo. I just forgot to remember that she was one of our rich members! (Rich! Shades of Mrs. Hoyt and John D.!) She is to me— well, the *Priscilla* of her, first of all; everybody knows what that is. Before I really knew her—after my first meeting with her at the Farm, when she was up for a Thanksgiving or week-end, I *wanted* her. I was always making up to her mentally, and by and by I was doing it actually, and her conquest was complete. Since I began to share with her the bigger things—which means the harder things—I have always wanted her right in every council meeting for which I was responsible. One of the many things that makes her such a comfort is her *accessibility.* The three doors to her little house have always seemed to me to symbolize that, and the way the house sits right on the ground—just walk in and you'll find Priscilla. Even if the architect suggested the three doors and the right-there-on-the-level plan, it was because it was to be Priscilla's house: he was mystically influenced by that fact.

So what? I love Priscilla and I want her in all my committees and I forgot to remember that she might have a little money that she hadn't. . . . [missing 2 pages]

Returning from my walk, all in the dark last Friday night, I was drawn to the living room, where I sat for a long time, listening to the clock— Agnes's clock—as I have done so many times during the years of my residence with you all, after all the house was still. The fireplace was black but some unquenched life in the buried embers whispered an accompaniment to the clock. Long, long thoughts—thoughts that failed to rise to prayer, but that did count, afterwards. . . . Then the clock struck the hour for me. Surely for me, for no one else was listening. Midnight, by Agnes's clock; and the hidden fire still murmured. How I have treasured every little thing that Agnes has shared with me of her wifely experience, even such a public fact as that the beloved clock was Brother Will's first wedding anniversary gift to her! . . . And then I went to bed—and squirmed at the thought of Priscilla! The sublime and the ridiculous very close indeed in the linked moments of that farewell evening.

I had no intention of using that word, *farewell.* A true word that spoke itself. For I shall never come to the Farm again after the same fashion as my comings up to this last one. I shall come—to visit briefly, to live, if God will permit it; but it will be after a new fashion. It may have been on the train, when I woke up after a more or less uncomfortable nap, or it may have been later—Saturday, Sunday: I don't really know when, when I realized that my last visit has had a quite unexpected effect. It has driven me more deeply in on myself. On God, that means. That is good. I *have* been a lame duck, clinging, clinging, though not in the fashion our superficial critics think. I have complained of the desert-loneliness of my life. A sojourn in the desert is what I need. I take up my solitary life willingly now, and when I come to you again it will be after the new fashion.

83. To Agnes Gould [GF]   Wollaston, Mass.
                                             February 23, 1930

Dear home folks:

I beg to report:

From my scalp to my toes, from the epidermis inward to my marrow, and outward to my sensations, with machinery fearfully and wonderfully made, they have searched me and known me, from Wednesday to Saturday, at the hospital, and found me flawless. I am whole—I am perfect: a perfect 48!

I am discharged—to a convalescent home. Absurd, isn't it? when there's nothing to convalesce from. I am to have three weeks more of very complete rest, and then report to Dr. Means. Miss Barbour, of Miss Cannon's department, will help me make a final choice tomorrow, from a list of rest homes which we looked over yesterday. They have quite attractive places less expensive, and in one or two other respects more suitable, than Woodside Cottages. I had to take a couple of days between, to get an urgent dental filling and do a bit of urgent shopping. It will be two months next week since I went away for *one week's* vacation. I was not fitted out for a long absence, or for a lay-abed life.

Dears, I must not write as much as it would be necessary in order to tell you fully how lovely the M.G.H. [Massachusetts General Hospital] people were to me those three days. Just in a few breathless sentences, I can say that I was treated like royalty. Dr. Means had me in a private room, and looked in on me, in such a cordial way—like Caroline or Minnie tucking you in with a hot water bag: all that tenderness that forgets nothing—even during the periods when I was in the hands of other doctors and technicians. Miss Cannon or Miss Barbour called twice every day, with a rose or a message or an offer to do errands and what not. The librarian made a special trip to my room with her book wagon. And they would not let me pay a cent—that was the plan. But I told Miss Cannon about Elizabeth Chace's valentine, and after a little argument she allowed me a small share, the laboratory fees, amounting to seventeen dollars. (That, I believe, was a reduced rate, too). So that's all it cost me to find out that I am not diseased but merely tired (and I have a thesis on the subject, for some other time). There were also, of course, taxi fares and railroad fares and all the little extras that one allows one's self when one is wobbly and can't lift a suitcase unaided etc. or miss a lunch etc. Woodside was twenty dollars for five days. I am telling you all this so you'll better appreciate the magic of my valentine check, that bought so many helpful items for me.

Miss Cannon, Miss Barbour, Dr. Means are all to be inscribed in our book of love and remembered in our prayers. This whole business of my unfounded decrepitude is turning out one more adventure in friendship. I can only wonder where I would be floundering now, and how, if you hadn't suggested Miss Cannon. I shall underscore Agnes Gould's name once more in my individual book of love.

There's just one fly in the ointment of Dr. Means' moderate prescription: he does not wish me to write at present. Creative work isn't done in cold blood, and he doesn't like me all stirred up. I confess that prohibition falls heavily on me. I am all tuned to write—and how I need to see some money of my own earning!

Couldn't I go into the Mitebox again in April, with a basket on a pulley to haul me up and down, and haul firewood and water until warm weather and outdoor bathing? For I must be with my papers and my books; I must be, must be writing.

If you ever hear from a Mr. Giles, he's a young reverend gentleman interested in evangelical work, and studying psychology a bit in order to understand the emotional mechanism on which he is playing. He knew Marion Lewis at Worcester—was taking the same course—and is now doing a bit at M.G.H. He called on me in the hospital to hear more about Gould Farm. I gave him the most valuable word I had for him, which was that he should plan the rest of his course so as to include a few weeks at Gould Farm.

I will not allow myself another sheet—I mustn't.

84. To Thomas A. Watson [BP]   Ward Sea
                                      Red Hook, N.Y.
                                      June 6, 1933

Dear good friend:

Every once in a while you shame me, by showing me that I still have to learn the depth and purity of your sympathies, that know no barriers in any direction. Now it is your reception of my clumsy account of Baba's recent stirring in our lives. Why I thought it might chill you? I felt the extremity of our surrender to Baba, as I tried to report to you of his hold on us. Your own relation to him is so detached, I thought you might find us tiresome. But you came back with "gratitude" for my letter, and a renewal of your acceptance in "terms of your own philosophy," of what in our lives is the outstanding, all-transforming personal-impersonal bond.

Jo is still in the city. I am sending on your letters to her. Too good to miss.

Your letter of May 31st was here when I returned from the city. I was happy to learn that Gould Farm had enjoyed the delight of a visit from you and Elizabeth. Did you learn anew how they love and respect you?

You say "I missed you sadly at the Farm." That word was a comfort to me. I don't want to be forgotten as a part of Gould Farm. I think you know that there is always a welcome for us there; often comes an urgent invitation, repeated especially when they think we're up against it. As long as we can manage by any other dodge, it seems right to stay away; because they have so many helpless people to feed and shelter, and, too, people as old in the work as Jo and I can't come and go without causing a good deal of dislocation. Even in a short visit we'd be bound to get deep in the work, and then, perhaps when we were involved in intricate matters, one or both of us might be called away on Baba's business. To use Gould Farm as a convenience is something neither Jo nor I can willingly do. So we continue to dodge that wide-open door.

On June 4th you write about Baba's photograph, which Mr. Stokes proposes to broadcast. Do you know, I felt about it just as you do, after the first flush of pleasure at seeing a new picture of Baba. I am going to hope that some new intuition will cause Graham Stokes to restrict the distribution of this photo to friends. He seems to do all the things by intuition. I do not feel free to make any suggestion to him.

Thank you for all your good letters.

Love to you both.

You have said nothing for a long time about your painting. Are you doing anything?

85. To Agnes Gould [GF]

Boston, Mass.
January 27, 1935

Dear Agnes:

I am making a very special effort to get this to you by the hand of our dear Mrs. Morgan, because I stupidly left my address book in an office down town yesterday and I haven't Isabel's address by heart. Since Mrs. Morgan is going to tell you that I did not come in to see her off because I have a cold, I want you to know that I am having the best care—gallons of fruit juice and an osteopath on the way. Also you ought to know that I am too happy about the way things have been moving lately to mind a little thing like a cold.

I enclose a copy of my follow-up letter to Miss Hyams, which in itself will give you some idea of how the interview went. Although I am not presenting you with a cash contribution on the spot, I do feel very happy over the promise of this contact. Miss Hyams is a very simple, direct, uncomplicated person, and from all I know she is not laced up in any philanthropy-dispensing machinery. I believe she is entirely free to act on her own convictions. The warmth and simplicity of her response to my story makes me feel safe to predict that it is only necessary for her to be exposed for a few days to Gould Farm, and she will roll up her sleeves and help us dig. When towards the end of my story she asked me with amazing innocence "what is it you want," I replied, "we want you to come and visit us and see for yourself." In her acceptance of that invitation there was nothing perfunctory. She was expansive and twinkling about it. When she heard that we all worked, she said with enthusiasm "I'll cook, I love to cook." When I said "I know just where we will put you—in a lovely cottage down by the brook," she protested, "Oh no, I don't want to be in a cottage by myself"—intimating she wanted to be with the bunch. I suggested she should bring a friend or two, or a carload; she said "I'll bring a friend, I know somebody who will be interested."

I took as a favorable omen the quiet dignity with which she heard my protest that I did not want to hear any more that Jewish philanthropy was not supporting Gould Farm adequately. (I hope there is nothing scandalous in the way I turn Jew on occasion. Seriously, as a Jewish member of the staff I have felt sensitive about the matter.)

I shall take my time about getting over this cold. I see where I shall reap an unjust reward by being detained in Boston until Mrs. Morgan's return. The storm prevented me from attending her Thursday morning meditation class. If I manipulate my cold skillfully I shall be here another Thursday with a good conscience. Certainly one can't linger unnecessarily away from home with a good conscience.

Lester Perkins is doing this for me on the type writer as the kink in my spine does not like to write letters. Will you please forward this letter to the folks at home, also the enclosure.

I am thankful to hear you have had your talk with Dr. Reed and that you feel satisfied with the results.

When you have posted Dr. Burr, all the loose ends in regard to Edna Somah will have been tied up.

I suppose you will have to wait to write to Mr. Winslow until he has made the first official move.

It will amuse you to know that having lost Isabel's address I am sending Harry Perkins in to the South Station to find Mrs. Morgan, whom he does not know, to get her to carry this letter to you.

> Love to you and best wishes.

86. To Agnes Gould [GF]   Boston, Mass.
                                                     January 6, 1936

Dear Agnes et al:

Yesterday—Epiphany Sunday evening I went to St. Paul's for the Service of Lights. The church was full, the service beautifully carried out. I was reminded of the simplicity of my duty: to seek the Light, to cherish the Light, to pass on the Light. All else is outside my responsibility.

Dr. Taylor has undertaken to help find me a cook-secy; why not. I told her about the check from home. She appreciates it all. It is not only poetical, it is constitutional: "Purpose of the W.J.G. Co., Inc.," paragraph 2: *Beneficiaries may be assisted away from the community.*

> Love to you all,

Mary Antin in 1914

CHAPTER FIVE

The Last Years

1937–1949

Obscurity and illness marked Antin's last years. Friends and acquaintances from her famous past had long since abandoned her. She renewed contact briefly with Ellery Sedgwick, her former editor at the *Atlantic Monthly,* writing to him twice in March 1937. The first letter is a condolence note on the death of his wife and includes very telling words about her own loss. "I have known sunderings more cruel than death," she lamented.* But ten days later she wrote a joyous letter informing him that her long-estranged husband, Amadeus Grabau, was to receive a national honor for his work in paleontology and she was to be his proxy in Washington, D.C. How curious it is that the tone of the letter is as though the Grabaus' marriage had endured normally instead of resulting in nearly twenty years of separation. (Four years earlier, in 1933, Grabau participated in the Sixteenth International Geological Congress in Washington, D.C., but there is no evidence that he contacted Antin or his daughter during his stay.) The last letter to Sedgwick reveals the abiding affection Antin had for her husband, and it gives us an insight into what must have been an enduring and painful loss of his companionship.

Although Antin had virtually no contact with her former friends, in 1934 she received a letter from Rabbi Abraham Cronbach.† He and his congregation had hosted Antin in South Bend, Indiana, in 1916 when she was on a speaking tour against the restrictive immigration policy about to be en-

---

*Antin to Sedgwick, Mar. 9, 1937.

†Abraham Cronbach (1882–1965), an American Reform rabbi, author, and teacher, served as rabbi at Beth El Temple in South Bend, Indiana (1906–1915), and under Rabbi Stephen Wise at the Free Synagogue in New York (1915–1917). Cronbach taught social studies at Hebrew College (1922–1950) and was an early proponent of involving the synagogue in community social action. He befriended the convicted murderer Nathan Leopold

acted in Congress. Later that same year, Cronbach was a guest at Antin's Hanukkah party in Scarsdale. Recalling the event in his 1959 autobiography, Cronbach wrote, "By then [Antin] had abandoned the antipathy to Jewishness which was described in *The Promised Land*."* Cronbach remembered that among the guests were professional singers and celebrities and that Antin herself had a beautiful voice. In the mid-1930s the rabbi learned that Antin had been hospitalized earlier, then had served on a hospital staff (Gould Farm, presumably). He began to send her yearly Jewish New Year greetings. However, three years passed before Antin responded, and in 1937 an extraordinary correspondence began that, in addition to being a yearly restatement of their friendship, served as an important forum in which Antin could express her interests in religious beliefs, ask questions about spiritual matters, and air her ideas about mysticism. She relied on Cronbach's knowledge of Jewish texts for answers to some of her questions, and perhaps, also, she used the rabbi's resolute commitment to Judaism as a standard against which to measure her many religious and mystical views.

The nearly two dozen letters they exchanged are an excellent chronicle of the subjects that occupied Antin's thoughts during this period of declining health. Cronbach's was a voice from the past, a past that differed greatly from the sad and lonely life she now led. The warm ties that Antin and Cronbach forged in 1916 remained intact during the twenty years in which Antin's name disappeared from the public domain.

In this last decade of her life, Antin became increasingly spiritual, as though a realistic look back on her life would be too painful. From the Cronbach letters, we learn that Antin incorporated some of the Christian ideas she had become acquainted with at Gould Farm into her Jewish identity. Immersing herself in various religions and philosophies became a way of coping. She was dealing with loneliness and mental and physical illness, and also with a sense of helplessness in knowing that Europe's Jews were in mortal danger while she remained safe in America. The gathering storm in Europe, as it affected European Jewry, was always on her mind, and she identified with them and their suffering. "Don't let me make any parenthetical allusions to the situation in Europe," she wrote. "I have moments of poise and hours of raw agony."†

---

and was rabbi to the convicted spies Ethel and Julius Rosenberg. He supported the anti-Zionist Council for Judaism opposing the use of Hebrew in American Jewish religious life.

*Abraham Cronbach. 1959. "Autobiography," *American Jewish Archives* 3, no. 4 (Apr.): 40–43.

†Antin to Cronbach, Dec. 5, 1938.

In the 1940s, Antin became especially enamored of Rudolph Steiner's writings. Steiner espoused a new philosophy and method of esoteric and spiritual teaching called anthroposophy. Some of his work focused on the supersensible world, a world he reported was accessible to him from the age of eight when he experienced a discarnate form of a recently deceased relative.* One principle of anthroposophy—that by virtue of a prescribed method of self-discipline, a perception of the spiritual world could be achieved—appealed to Antin greatly. She was very eager to share her new preoccupation, writing several times to Cronbach about Steiner to engage the rabbi's interest. Although religious belief is a matter of faith, the imprimatur of science upon Christianity and the occult as proposed by Steiner caused Antin's free-floating ideas about spiritual matters to gel into what she believed to be her "destiny." Whether Steiner's ideas would have sustained Antin's keen attention indefinitely we cannot know, as she died within three years of her burgeoning interest.

Antin died in 1949 while in her sister Clara's care, and is buried with her sisters and brother in the family plot in the Hartsdale, New York, Mount Pleasant cemetery.

87. To Ellery Sedgwick [MH]   42 South Russell Street
                                              Boston, Mass.
                                              March 9, 1937

My dear Mr. Sedgwick:
    Please accept my profound sympathy on your great bereavement. I have known sunderings more cruel than death, nevertheless I feel deeply for all who have to lose what death comes to claim.

                                              Sincerely yours,

88. To Ellery Sedgwick [MH]   42 South Russell Street
                                              Boston, Mass.
                                              March 19, 1937

Dear Mr. Sedgwick:
    That was a precious word you sent me on the little card. I wish I might have known Mrs. Sedgwick. My one glimpse of her was the oblique image in your most amusing *Tale of New Japan*!

*Seddon 1988.

"In death we are not divided." What a victory to be able to say that! And what an adventure all of it is: the groping we call life, with its occasional flashes of illumination that compensate and assure us.

Thank you, thank you for your good word.

Sincerely,

You will appreciate this bit: I go to Washington on April 27th as my husband's proxy to receive a medal awarded to him, "for most important services to geology and palaentology," of the National Academy of Sciences. The flavor of melodrama is in the thing, but I have a deep substantial joy in the event. He has so heroically labored without thought of reward.

89. To Abraham Cronbach [AJA]

42 South Russell Street
Boston, Mass.
May 17, 1937

My dear Dr. Cronbach:

Let this word from me, at a moment when you have given up all expectation of any response to your several communications, be a symbol to you of the absolute spiritual value of a friendly act, irrespective of the worth of the beneficiary or of his capacity to respond. Again and again— at the New Year of 1934, 1935, 1936—you sent a good word my way, and you only restrained your expression the third time because you have received no sign to indicate that your messages were welcome.

See, I will pay you the great compliment of assuming that you are one of those who can dispense with excuses, with explanations; who hold out their cup to receive the wine of friendship undiluted with the small distrusts, the egoistical demands and anxieties that in others have to be healed with apology and self-abasement. But did I say *assume?* I *know:* it is guaranteed by the spontaneity of your first letter and the generosity of your repeated attempts to reach me, in spite of my silences.

In your gracious allusions to your visit to my home in Scarsdale, now twenty years ago, you gave me back, for an hour, all the good things that home stood for. I was touched by the vividness of your recollections: you seemed to be saying to me that what was astir in that home—which indeed was shared with many—must be immortal, to have left so strong an impression on a thoughtful, sensitive visitor like you. If I ever forget what the Scarsdale home was like, I shall run to you! You remind me that some one very wise has said that whatever is good, is permanent.

"The war was hard on me," you say in one place—just as a matter of record, I note; not as a complaint. Well, the war was hard on me, too, and I was not exactly in your camp, though I found my way there afterwards. The war swept away the home in Scarsdale—all except what still abides in invisible form, such as your kind remembrance of it. And "many vicissitudes" followed, of course. My best schooling: if I am in any sense a civilized creature today, it is because the years brought me precious chastisement. I have been to school to sorrow and pain, with the result that I have discerned something of the beauty of the Lord and the joy of his salvation.

The lines from Isaiah which you quote in your 1934 letter—

> In returning and rest shall ye be saved;
> In quietness and in confidence shall be your strength—

they have been very familiar and dear to me from a good while back. Meditating on these lines, I once made a little pastel painting, an abstract color design that seemed to carry the spirit of that saying, judging from what friends have said of it when given a chance to interpret it unprompted. (No, I am not a painter; I do play with pastels.) I am not at all curious to know what intimations have reached you as to my latter years; I am grateful for the generous interpretation you have put upon the rumors.

With many thanks for your loyal friendship, and all good wishes for yourself, your little family, and your fine work,

Sincerely yours,

The Hanukkah friends, whose singing you recall, were Mr. & Mrs. Henry Gideon. Mr. Gideon has been choirmaster & organist at Temple Israel, Boston, all these years.

90. To Abraham Cronbach [AJA]

MacDowell Colony
Peterborough, N.H.
September 4, 1937

My dear Dr. Cronbach:

I welcome all your kind personal words and appropriate the good teaching of the words of Isaiah which you quote with such fine appreciation, in your letter of September 1. We appear to be very close in our view of God's world in its current moment. I, too, am much occupied with the realization of the constructive forces at work in the midst of the more obvious horror and Terror. The sanity of the cosmic order triumphs over all our momentary insanities—"Yea, I have a goodly heritage," is my daily confession.

All best wishes to you in the New Year. All power to do your part in shaping the New Age which humanity is entering.

Cordially,

You will be interested, I think, in an essay I had in the *Atlantic Monthly* for May.

91. To Abraham Cronbach [AJA]

115 Granger St.
Wollaston, Mass.
October 7, 1938

Dear friend:

Your choice New Year greeting, so deep in its thought and so beautiful in expression came to me at a moment of low ebb, physically and morally, and recharged my batteries at the first reading. (Indeed I have read it more than once.) I was just out of the hospital, trying to teach myself to walk again, and my small gains in energy were being offset by the terrific blows of reports from the cauldron that was Europe during the last week of September. Like the sound of the *Shofar* itself, your serene sentences recalled me to those things that are eternal, that outlast and outweigh all the works of men that have their springs in folly.

Ah, yes, "the deeper blessings of life's losses"—it is they that make for sanity and faith. Always, when I have been most broken by suffering, has risen in my heart the irrepressible acknowledgement, *How excellent is the loving kindness, O God!*

Gratefully, and with all best wishes for you and yours,

92. To Margaret Prescott Montague [WV]

Gould Farm
Great Barrington, Mass.
November 5, 1938

Dear Miss Montague:

Again I recall myself to your attention, after one of the long dead silences that has interrupted my contacts with people and things that mean life to me. Illness—more of it—I am ashamed to report. I really am a robust person, fundamentally: I just trip over time-devouring accidents now and again. And here am I at one of my optimistic new beginnings!

I have at hand another small essay on the same subject as the "Trumpet" piece about which we have corresponded. The *Atlantic* has waited for it for a year. This time, under title "Arise from the Dead!" I try to indicate that inner states such as that first article described are, as you and I agree—yes, I quote you: I have to—increasingly common, and I attempt to set out in words of one syllable, so to speak, the meaning of such phenomena, following Bucke and his school in this part of the argument. The "moral" of this piece is found in some suggestion of what the average earnest man, initiated or not, can do to promote the development of this natural benevolent force in human affairs.

Would you care to read this paper—about 6,000 words, I estimate—and make suggestions? I would send you a copy at the same time as it goes to the *Atlantic,* so I can have the benefit of all criticisms at once. I am so aware of being the fool who rushes in, in venturing on this subject, that I cannot neglect any possible correction available. And there is no one I would trust more than you in the place of critic.

My little piece was begun over a year ago, but it is only within the month that I was able to assemble the reading matter I needed for reference. Besides Bucke, whom I know from years back, I have, now, the *Modern Mystics* of Younghusband, for which I have you to thank—you recommended it in one of your letters. I have also just come across the English Dr. Hall's *Observed Illuminates,* very much to the point too. Can this be the book you referred to when you said (Aug. 25, 1937), "There is an English doctor who has just completed a book on Illumination"? But Hall's book appeared in 1926. (I am not exactly famous for my typing!) I am well acquainted with Evelyn Underhill and others you mention; Ouspensky *(Tertium Organum* and *A New Model of the Universe)* has been most illuminating. And pointing to the relevance of the mystic states and practices to the present needs of society, I have profited by Aldous Huxley, *Ends and Means,* Gerald Heard, *The Third Morality,* and Herbert Martin, *A Philosophy of Friendship.* Also the compact exposition of the tendency to world unity in *A Modern in Search of Truth* by S. T.—whose anonymity I hope to pierce.

Is it your judgment that I have neglected any important contemporary writing that I should call to further witness? Perhaps you cannot judge in advance of seeing my paper.* In the meantime, I wish I could get at your own work in fiction form, the stories, and the *Leaves from a Secret Jour-*

*"Arise from the Dead!" (Antin's footnote)

nal. I think I can get old files of the *Atlantic* if you will be good enough to give me the dates. And where is the novel?—I have also done a short story on illumination, perhaps good enough to be worth revising presently.

To the family at Gould Farm you are more than ever an important person and a congenial spirit. Mrs. Gould and one or two others have recently been drawn into the family of the mystics—at least they stand on the threshold in desire to enter in. You are often quoted ("Twenty Minutes"). This new development makes me happy; for long I was rather alone here in my less orthodox spiritual life. Lest you credit me with these new developments at the Farm, I must tell you that it occurred during the last three years, when I joined the group only for the shortest visits. Of course in a group like this we affect one another's growth in one way and another. I only know that when I first came buzzing in their ears about my less orthodox excursions I was treated with affectionate sympathy and the most ungrudging tolerance, but our paths for a while diverged. It was my privilege to present the family with a copy of your "Twenty Minutes" at the time you thought of coming here, but it is only now the book has really been appropriated by the circle. Is not this an indication that you really must come home to us at last?

In any and all events, I am indebted to you. Gratefully then,

Your friend on the way toward new horizons,

93. To Margaret Prescott Montague [WV]
Gould Farm
Great Barrington, Mass.
November 22, 1938

Dear Miss Montague:

That was a generous letter you wrote me on the 8th. A helpful one, too. And it made Mrs. Gould happy to know that I am freshly in touch with you.

Mrs. Gould sends you Thanksgiving greetings, with thanks for what you are, just *as* you are—with all the infirmities you think to frighten us with! In a sense we are a community of the infirm and the Farm is a repair shop or refreshment station. Therein is both our job and our resource. By pooling our lacks we pool our riches, and all are the better endowed in the end. There is no waste here: odds and ends of gifts, remnants of health and faint sparks of inspiration, latent talents and disregarded spiritual forces—the broken pieces left over from the bountiful feast of our so-called better days, all these, collected together and consecrated to mutual service, afford us ample supply for our daily living, with a surplus to send out into the world.

Your sight is dim? There is someone here who will grow by reading to you the sort of books you need to keep up with. Your hearing is poor? We all aspire to grow in patience, and we have, actually, one woman who makes it a practice to repeat, for lip-readers, what is said by the leader in our prayer meeting etc. One frequent guest to whom many confessedly have owed inspiration is a woman deaf, dumb, and blind. One of the most entertaining teams we ever had was, a few years ago, a woman totally deaf and a man crippled from infancy. But these are the obvious cripplings: we draw more of inspiration and courage, yes, and growth in skill, from the many whose lacks are more serious for being less visible, in wrestling with whose problems we come ever a little nearer to understanding the spiritual laws of health and work.

And we know, all of us, that "not always on the mountain heights" is the rule of the ascent. No, we wouldn't expect to see you come to breakfast every morning with a halo of illumination! We really are a lot of sensible people. When you have come to a moment that sets your heart toward Gould Farm, there will be a welcome for you without the penalty of unreasonable expectations to meet.

Shall I go back to my essay for a moment? Of course I would not want my reports of my own insights edited. Only in my attempt to explicate, to point a "moral," have I been a little diffident. I hold myself subject to correction there. Correction no doubt will come from my readers. The *Atlantic* has the essay now, but I haven't heard whether it's accepted—it was submitted, as usual, for approval.

I take special delight in the knowledge that you and I are dividing between us the text from Ephesians, as titles for our two pieces! Now have I your poem to look forward to. I have read far too little of what you have written. To date I haven't got hold of your stories in the *Atlantic* of long ago, but I have sent for the *Leaves*—how good of you to let me know where to get it.

Hebrew Mysticism—yes, that is a rich field. I don't think I am in any way better qualified to introduce it to the world than you are. Don't wait for me; go ahead, do it yourself, and if in any way I can help, only let me know.

With best wishes,

                                        Cordially yours,

94. To Abraham Cronbach [AJA]   Gould Farm
Great Barrington, Mass.
November 26, 1938

Dear Dr. Cronbach:

I come asking your help this time. For the second of a series of three essays on the *second birth** or awakening to *cosmic consciousness* (the first of which series was published in the *Atlantic Monthly* for May, 1937, under title "The Soundless Trumpet"), I am using a line from Ephesians for a title: "Arise from the Dead" (Eph. 5:14). As I wish to convey, in an introductory motto, the universality of the teaching in all scriptures, I am taking a passage from the Sufi poet Kabir expressing the same thought as the passage from Ephesians, to which I wish to add also a corresponding word from Hebrew mystical sources. I have no books at hand, no good library within reach. Besides, I am too ignorant of Hebrew mystical literature to know where to look! Jewish mysticism of the Middle Ages has long attracted me, from hints and intimations received in my Ghetto childhood, but I have done almost nothing to follow those clues. It occurred to me that you may have at your finger ends—or on the tip of your tongue, I suppose I should have said—what I am looking for.

The passage from Ephesians is familiar. Kabir may not be among our familiars—I was introduced to him not more than six years ago. I subjoin the passage taken from the "Songs" (XIX), translations by Tagore (Macmillan Company):

> O my heart! the Supreme Spirit, the great Master
> is near you: wake, oh wake!
> Run to the feet of your Beloved: for your
> Lord stands near to your head.
> You have slept for unnumbered ages; this
> morning will you not wake?

It will give me great pleasure to have your assistance in this matter. The essay may be going to press very soon—I expect word from the *Atlantic* any day.

With best wishes,

Sincerely yours,

*Cosmic Consciousness goes far beyond "second birth," [illegible] which is usually understood to mean only inversions within the narrower sense. (Antin's footnote)

Strange how we are able to go about our private business in a time of culminating anguish for the Jews of the world, a time of peril for democracy. Not without stumbling, to be sure, but still keeping each one in his customary track. I wrote a small thing, hinging, in timing and structure, on the Thanksgiving season, but I was too late for publication. That's my answer to the roll call of those who understand and care, and it's left in my private file, alas.

95. To Elvie Wachenheim* [CZ]

Gould Farm
Great Barrington, Mass.
November 29, 1938

Dear Elvie,

I let twenty-four hours pass before acknowledging your letter. Death has visited me many times; I thought I knew how it felt to lose a friend. But this is—Jessie, Elvie, dear, I have been lost in a cloud of selfish grief. I can't *spare* Jessie. I believe that you, who know how little contact I had with her for a stretch of years, will nevertheless know how I can say that. I had such a good feeling when I sent off that letter which never reached her, that there was before us a new era of close communication. I have hopes that my life is going to follow more orderly lines now, for as long as it might last; and one of those things I expected order to yield me was the satisfaction of regular exchanges with Jessie.

How beautifully she fulfilled all her major undertakings! She wasted nothing of her talents. Every gift she had, all her energy, was constantly in use, fully integrated with her main purpose. She was such a substantial person in all her relationships. No loose ends, no raveled edges. Her honesty of mind was even more impressive than her originality. With all the passion for the cause she gave most to, you always knew you could depend on her for an unprejudiced report of events, an interpretation not colored by her wishes. Her development as a force in Jewish life went far beyond Josephine Lazarus's prediction. I think I'll sit down and learn Hebrew just for the sake of tasting Jessie's expression of herself in that grand language. There, I am sure, I'd find still another Jessie. I have always felt very humble before her—and how she'd so laugh at that! So whole, so free in the

---

*Elvie Wachenheim was Jessie Sampter's sister. Mary Antin's granddaughter Anne Ross remembers Elvie's generosity and thoughtfulness when, during an impoverished youth, packages containing luxurious gifts of beautiful bathrobes and elegant dolls arrived at Christmas from Mrs. Wachenheim.

freedom one has to win for one's self, so prolific in outgoing affections, so full of charity and tenderness and whimsy, her intellectual integrity shot through with the warm light of tolerance. I seldom remembered that she had physical handicaps to overcome; attention was always diverted to that triumphal quality in all her doings, as if failure could never bar her path. Best of all I like to remember her devotion to all the *little* people she befriended, the socially unimportant, the poor in heart and in goods and in station.

It's to Elvie I'm writing, so I don't pick my words. Dear Elvie! You've been such a wonderful sister to her! And now Tamar is left, and it's a happy thing that she renewed contact with you so recently. I know how much the relationship must mean to her at this time.

I know you will write to me all there is to write as you get time.

I sent word to Jo, as you requested.

Thank you, dear Elvie, for writing me so promptly.

And love to you.

96. To Abraham Cronbach [AJA]

Gould Farm
Great Barrington, Mass.
December 5, 1938

Dear friend:

I am most grateful! I like a partnership with you, and I like the quotation. But I can't stop with the brief quotations—which I might have known in advance. Will you give me the references to the Judah Halevi and the Alkabez works you quoted from?* I may be able to get them from the Boston Public Library. Judah Halevi is a name I knew as a child in Poloztk, but the other is entirely new to me.

Another request: I want a book of Jewish legends, post-Biblical, available in English, for a Gentile boy of fourteen—who is very advanced in reading and who has recently become interested in the Jews (through the shock of things in Europe!). Also, a one-volume history of the Jews—need I say, non-sentimental and non-apologetic.

If it isn't pressing you too atrociously, I want to be able to get these books before Christmas. I am sending the same enquiry to my friend

---

*Judah Ha-Levi (c. 1080–c. 1140), a Spanish rabbi, poet, and philosopher, born in Toledo, Spain, is considered the most outstanding poet of the golden period of Hebrew letters. A physician by profession, he possessed a profound knowledge of biblical and rabbinic literature.

Fanny Goldstein of the Boston Public Library (West End Branch).* Between you two, I should get right guidance.

Don't let me make any parenthetical allusions to the situation in Europe. I have moments of poise and hours of raw agony. Forgive me for saying this much.

Sincerely,

97. To Abraham Cronbach [AJA]

Cohasset, Mass.
September 29, 1939

Dear Dr. Cronbach:

How precious is friendship in a world of terror and treachery! Your New Year message was more than ever comforting for the background of current conditions in the world, and also because it found me in a middle stage of convalescence from a serious operation. I thank you for every word of it.

Cohasset is on the South Shore of Massachusetts, a picturesque bit of the coast that I have long loved. Here in a sandy cove curving between bare granite cliffs, I have found quiet and sunshine and the tonic of sea bathing. My days are still checkered with a convalescent's ups and downs, but I begin to come to life. I begin, almost, to think!—whereas for the last eight weeks I have just barely reconnoitered the fringe of response to what I read in the prayers and hear from the radio.

By terrible things in righteousness God makes himself known, today as always. It is wonderful to wake up these mornings and realize that though the earth melt, Truth—God—is unshaken.

All best wishes to you in the New Year.

Gratefully,

98. To Abraham Cronbach [AJA]

Threefold Farm
Spring Valley, N.Y.
December 20, 1940

Dear friend:

In return for the illuminating messages, annually renewed, in your own original voice, I can do no less than introduce to you another voice, one

---

*Fanny Goldstein (1888–1961), a librarian at the West End Branch of the Boston Public Library, started the Jewish Book Week in 1930 and became curator of Judaica at the library in 1954.

which has given full answers to the deeper questions I have sought through all my mature years. If you are already acquainted with Rudolf Steiner, you will understand the prompting to bring him upon the scene of our occasional intercourse. You know what things have most concerned me; you will understand what my responses to this teaching or that break through much travail of soul. Whether Rudolf Steiner rouses any responsive echo in your heart—whether positive or negative—you will still sympathize with this imfoldment in my life, because your spirit is friendly and tolerant in the best sense.

Another new year overlaps the years behind us. The world is in extremity of revolution. The face of the world to come only the prophets have seen. I take my watch as you do, in the sure places of the Holy Spirit.

Cordially,

99. To Abraham Cronbach [AJA]

Threefold Farm
Spring Valley, N.Y.
September 21, 1941

My dear friend:

I welcome with gratitude your annual visit in spirit. Your words of faith and vision I always share with a few friends near at hand—they are too choice to file away unshared.

I appreciate also your faithfulness in personal friendship all these long, scarred, illumined years. Shall we meet again, do you suppose? I don't know that I would be the richer for a meeting: you have so well communicated your best, in your recurrent New Year epistles.

All best wishes of the season,

100. To Abraham Cronbach [AJA]

Gould Farm
Great Barrington, Mass.
March 20, 1943

Dear Friend:

It is usually half way down the year when I respond to your faithful and ever welcome New Year greeting. I shall strive to be born again a better correspondent than I have been in my present life span. I am not deficient in love and appreciation of the friends God has given me, but I consistently let them suffer from my unreliability as a correspondent.

No matter how many months after its receipt I reread one of your New Year letters, I always recapture the warmth and poignancy of your message. "Refuge and anchorage in the Eternal." Yes, that sums up the state my destiny has brought me to. I feel that you and I understand each other deeply on the basis of that long ago face-to-face meeting. Nevertheless I would be ready to go a good piece out of my way to talk with you again. For I have seen great and glorious things in the Lord—the Lord whom we may call by different names but who is still the same—of which I would like to tell you.

I was delighted to see your little article in the special issue of the *American Friend*. On the subject of saintliness, will you believe me if I tell you that in this Gould Farm circle, to which I have recently returned, are three of the saintliest beings I have ever known anywhere? They exhibit in daily life the authentic saintly pattern which you hold up in your article; so much so, that I hold myself responsible for systematic imitation of their ways.

I think when you last heard from me, I was at Threefold Farm. Almost twenty years ago my destiny in the form of illness brought me to Gould Farm. Now destiny, again in the same form, brings me back to Gould Farm. My heart isn't as good as it used to be, and at Threefold Farm, I couldn't get the pampering that's prescribed. So here I am back at my old stamping ground and thankful to be here. There is no sense of retreat in this return to Gould Farm: it is quite obviously the resumption of a pattern which *belongs*.

In the Gould Farm neighborhood are several fellow members of the Wider Quaker Fellowship. Their coming and going here is a source of satisfaction to me. I wish it were thinkable that your comings and goings might also bring you to us some day. With best wishes.

Cordially,

101. To Abraham Cronbach [AJA]   868 Lancaster Street
Albany 3, N.Y.
February 8, 1945

Dear Dr. Cronbach:

This is no anniversary, either private or public, not an "occasion" in any calendar sense, yet it is a day very special, because I am writing to my good friend to whom I write less than once a year, of whom I think the more often because I have a desire of the heart to be in communication with him and that desire I do not satisfy.

I have just reread, most thoughtfully, the last two of your dear annual letters to me: your New Year letters of 1943 and 1944. I file very few letters—I have lived for many years in a valedictory mood, not entirely because of failing health; and accordingly I study to avoid accumulation of matter for my survivors to labor over. *Your* letters are among those it costs something to consign to the fire. Every time you write you achieve a fresh impression of personal impact. How could you possibly bring me more of yourself, of your spirit, of your meaning in a personal visit? You let me see into the depths of your reflections on life; you furnish me every time with a revised map of your spiritual pilgrimage. That is the only "news" I want of my friends, as I have grown older: *how is it with you on the inner path?* Nevertheless, like yourself, I would dearly love a meeting face to face. As you have of course marked, I have said little—almost nothing—as to my latter-day discoveries, in my few letters. And there is much that I would like to share. So why don't you definitely plan to make an extension of your parochial circuit for my benefit? You have included me in your pastoral family by your annual letters. I do not travel now; you do. Make a side trip my way, say in the summer when I am at Gould Farm. (Albany is a winter camping ground, in a way. It has been too cold for me at Gould Farm winters, recently.)

Yes, of course I was once your teacher—because you are one of the rare sort who can learn of everybody. It is one of the life phenomena that should keep us alert, that the roles of teacher and pupil may be reversed from period to period. Let us, in any case, get together and learn together!

I have alluded in this letter to my practice of guarding against accumulations. I have gone farther than that, in recent years: I have been indulging in the pleasure of passing on items of my small remaining store of personal belongings to friends who may enjoy them. Just lately I had another session of pruning my library, much of which has already been distributed. I held in my hand an odd book, a tragic commentary in its very existence on the tragic history of the Jews, which I had bought in, with many other volumes, when the library of my friend Josephine Lazarus was sold, after her death, in 1911. The book had been through a fire before it came into my hands and has been water-damaged in another fire since (when my goods were in storage for a time). It has been skillfully repaired and bound by my brother-in-law, John Grabau. I enclose a copy of the title page for your perusal, as a basis for judging whether you would care to have this book as a keepsake from me. You are a scholar and teacher. You are bound to continue to collect, to possess books to the end, even if you should happen to have been bitten by the same bug of impatience at possessions that has bitten me. I ask you to accept this volume if it will not be a burden to you. By not sending the book, but only a description in the first instance, I mean to leave you free to decline the gift. But if you want it, it will give me joy to send it. I've had this book lying about in view for more than a week, ever since I had the thought "Send it to Dr. Cronbach! He may like to add it to his scholar's library."

Now let me add a word of congratulations on your daughter's marriage. We always say "congratulations," meaning good wishes. I have missed knowing your daughter by so little: it looked at one time as if she was on the point of making me a visit. Perhaps this marriage is really a case for congratulations. (I know one wartime marriage, quite mad in its origin, which is turning out a joy and satisfaction to all who are in contact with the two young people.) One falls into the error of thinking of a marriage announced in these days as a "wartime marriage." (Of course not all of them are that). In any case a daughter's marriage is an event of importance, a sort of turning point in the life of the parents. When your first grandchild arrives you will be close to my trail, humanly speaking. I am at this time awaiting my third. Yes, I have done my bit of grandmotherly knitting and all!

With renewed thanks for your ever-fresh, ever touching loyalty,

Your friend,

102. To Abraham Cronbach [AJA]

Brooklyn, N.Y.
March 4, 1945

Dear friend:

Your letter of the 18th of February has been forwarded to me on a visit to New York. It is good to know that there really is a possibility of a face-to-face visit with you! Albany? Gould Farm? Only keep me posted, and I'll do my part in taking advantage of your movements.

I am on the move myself, off and on, within a limited area. Usually visits to my excellent physician in N.Y.C. and incidental to these, visits to members of my family within easy reach of N.Y.C. So you have to give me ample notice of your advent. When away from my headquarters, I only have mail forwarded if my absence stretches over a week.

So I shall send on the antique volume, for you to dispose of as you see fit. Perhaps I'll send you also a list of other items of Judaica, in case you would be interested on behalf of the College library.

Thank you, thank you for a photo of your daughter with her husband. A charming young couple, surely—to be sure not all marriages of the hour are war marriages, but all young folks marrying at this time have the disordered conditions of the world to face. One needs to pray for them.

Cordially as ever,

We shall talk about your "creed," then—and about much else!

103. To Agnes Gould [GF]   Stone House
                                                October 3, 1945

Dear Agnes Gould:

In kindness to you I ought to make a careful draft, and from that a neat copy, of what I want to say on this occasion, but you who have forgiven me so much will forgive also the lengthiness and rambling style which I am afraid will mark this communication, done offhand on the type-writer—to save myself the extra effort—and under tension of a certain anxiety, which I shall name later, if I don't forget.

A while ago I made a beginning on the book we have all been waiting for, the story of Brother Will and Gould Farm. A small and halting begin-ning on which I do not ask anyone to pin too great hopes, nevertheless, a beginning. The reason I have not let you in on this is because I do not want to expose you to possible additional disappointments, after all you have suffered these many years through my delinquency. This, indeed, is the anxiety I referred to in my first paragraph, which has kept me hesitat-ing a good while on the point of writing this letter. You are having a rather rough time just now—a long siege of dentistry on top of the usual con-glomerate of problems and maybe crises. Is this a moment to get you all stirred up with a matter of such deep emotional content as this of the long-overdue, long-despaired-of book of Gould Farm? I would have pre-ferred to wait till I was further along—till I could put a fat portion of the manuscript into your hands. But I am going far away, if plans work out, for a good six months. I do not know when I would next get to talk with you—it *may* prove even more difficult to get together when I'm in Florida than it has these two months when I was within two miles of the Farm! I want to ask you now for those letters I didn't want to take out of your hands before, and perhaps line up some further co-operation that I long ago made a note of—things I didn't want anybody to spend time on, as long as I halted at my end. Please understand that I am not pressing for an interview—I can register my needs with Rose just as well; but of course it will be good to have a little talk about this and that if each of us can man-age to soft-pedal our common tendency to enthusiasm.*

Oct. 5. —That long break couldn't be helped. I was obliged to attend to a flock of details, mostly on the telephone, which fatigues me, in con-nection with arrangements for Florida that were held up till this late day at

---

*Rose McKee (1897–1985) was an original associate of Gould Farm and Antin's friend.

the far end. And I can do only so much in a day. This letter has been cooling on the typewriter while I rested from other exertions. At least now I know where I'm going—Winter Park, where excellent accommodations have been secured. Rose has offered to tote me in her car to Albany on Tuesday or Wednesday next, so I haven't very much time left in these parts.

I am tempted to give you a rather full history of my long ordeal of nonperformance, the counterpart of your ordeal—and "you" and "your" are plural, in this document. I must not spend my energy in this fashion. Some little I have to say, or the lifting of the icy silence will still leave too much mystery to tease you. Your speculations on this subject—for in absence of facts which I did not volunteer to give and your delicacy would not let you ask for, speculation was inevitable—I say in your speculations you may have come near the truth, which is that I was suffering from a deep soul sickness. The history of my too many external illnesses, known to you all in good part, tells only the lesser part. I have been sicker than all that, and have known it for many years. I do not claim to be wholly recovered now; I am sufficiently healed to be able to cast off the protective silence, and you will admit that is something.

To nobody did I speak of my deeper sickness until little over a year ago, when I consulted Dr. Winkler for the first time. No, that's not quite accurate, I just recollect, but I shall not further qualify my statement, which is *substantially* true. Certainly it is true that I took no personal friends into my confidence, on or off the Farm. Perhaps I would be farther along at this moment if, having made the contact with Dr. Winkler, I had stayed within reach of more systematic treatment. I did not see my way to do that until last spring, which is another way of saying I wasn't very intelligent in the matter. In any case it stands that I came to Dr. Winkler *a little late;* nevertheless he has helped me substantially in spite of interference of acute physical illness, which themselves were partly due to my delay in seeking treatment. Right here it occurs to me that I may be doing Dr. Winkler a disservice in thus hanging on him, so to speak, the outcome of this tardily inaugurated "cure." He is not a miracle worker; he *is* an exceptional physician, and to him I owe the blessedness of being enabled to make at least a beginning toward discharging some outstanding obligations which have weighed on me with the weight of doom these many years.

Here I am again touching the nature of the anxiety which kept me hesitating about divulging to you the facts of my small new beginning. I did come a little late to the physician who has enabled me to make this start, with the help of anthroposophic medical principles. We are none of us as young as we were when the project of this book was first sighted. There may be disappointment in the end. Why stir you up prematurely? But this risk, I suppose, is part of our inseparable suffering, yours and mine. We shared in the joy and expectation of the inception and growth of the project, we suffered through the long period of the gradual sinking into silence and inactivity—I in loneliness, the rest of you in joint bewilderment and mystification and embarrassment; and now that I am restored to inner life—just when I am outwardly less alive than at any time since you've known me!—I suppose it's inevitable that we should share whatever is about to result from my renewed endeavors. At any rate, I seem to have talked myself around to taking this risk.

I spoke, a little way back, of my self-protective silence. It is a common symptom of a certain type of person when under the blight of what it is the fashion to call psycho-neurosis. In my case I was quite conscious of what besides egoism enjoined this silence: I wouldn't expose myself to the inevitable well-meant meddling of solicitous friends, everyone with a different doctor, treatment, medicine man or what not to press upon the ailing one. One sees plenty of that so natural, so human endeavor everywhere in the world; one sees it in intensive form at our blessed Farm, understandably so; and I have done my share of this urging of pet cures on others. I deliberately shut myself off from that added harassment, while continuing the quest of the wise physician—not necessarily *qua* physician—in those ways that my nature allowed me.

You all know that I have a conscience. I sometimes wished it had atrophied somewhere along my long trek in the valley of the shadow of frustration. For it was an awful load for a tender conscience to carry, the sense of my delinquency. It was so logically my job, that book. All those years of growth of the Farm, and nobody else came who would do it. Brother Will had endorsed me, all the world that knew Gould Farm counted on me. And I had promised—promised first *myself;* and then tacitly, by taking people's time, so many people's time, on the Farm and far afield, to contribute what data they had for my book, I had promised a great many others.

Add to delinquency bankruptcy. For a long stretch of years I allowed the Farm to give me all sorts of exceptional privileges, in the way of housing especially—the choicest cottages and equipment—which I would have declined except that there was stirring in me this book-in-the-making, in connection with which it was indeed an advantage to have plenty of room for my books and so on, an agreeable setting for receiving visitors and conducting delicate interviews. I virtually let the Farm pay me in advance

for a job I never performed. True, I made certain good use of my privileged position in connection with the normal basic functioning of the
Farm, and some sort of "results" came from such use of what was loaned
me. But in my own consciousness—not, of course, in that of you others—
I was only justified in spreading myself out as I did because I was on a
special assignment, so to speak. Failing in my assignment—and what a
twisted, stealthy, half-blind process is the gradual realization of failure that
creeps up on you!—in my own eyes I was bankrupt.

But worst of all, most painful, most tormenting, was the steady consciousness of the suffering I was causing the rest of you. The mystification,
the sheer *embarrassment* before friends of the Farm. How is Mary Antin's
book coming along? Has she lost interest in the Farm? Can't you ask her?
I should think you have a right to ask. Is anything being done to conserve
the material she's been collecting? Isn't she on friendly terms with any of
you, so that you could at least know what the prospect is? I could go on
for a full page—describing easily imagined scenes, discussions, consulta-
tions in detail. For a major Gould Farm project had been stalled and you
bore a certain responsibility before the world, having innocently and justi-
fiably spread the word, or allowed it to be spread, that the story of Gould
Farm was to be given to the public. And you suffered not only from the
awkward position in which you were put, but also—how well I know it!—
from your concern for me, on account of the criticism I came under. I can
picture you torn between your loyalty to me personally and your responsibility to the public, as head of Gould Farm. (You will know, reading this,
when "you" is singular and when plural, though most of this applies to
the group.)

And now? Now I still have to ask that we all keep pretty quiet about
this thing. I am not asking you to make any promises. Your discretion and
common sense will tell you what will be proper in the circumstances. I will
just state that it would be no help to me to have too many people talking
about this. It is so much too soon. But you have borne restraints so long
and so patiently, I don't want to put restraint in a new form on you. I have
made a statement—I may yet add to it—and I'll abide by the conse-
quences of your interpretation of it.

There was a rest period here, and I find myself wanting to add something.

A while ago—more than a year, I think—I handed Rose McKee a small
fragment of the manuscript, with the request that it should not be circu-
lated. I didn't tell her why I showed her that bit, and I was, foolishly, disappointed that she didn't catch on—she'd have had to be clairvoyant to

get what my gesture meant! It's of no significance now, except that I learned anew that I am and have to be shy about anything I'm working on. It does something bad to me to imitate other writing people—the majority, I believe—who profit, somehow, by showing others what they're working on. Even with fellow craftsmen I'm just as shy—I found that out when I was at the MacDowell Colony. I don't know what I can do better than be myself in this funny business. So you can't expect much fun with the book while it's just getting under way. When I'm a good piece along, yes. Your marvelous patience will be getting another rib in its backbone (I wish I knew what this figure means!) Can do? The bit of the MS I showed Rose—and which she showed Sidney, on the principle, no doubt that they twain are one: but I had meant it wasn't to be shown to anybody at all: I have forgiven her—I will show it to you, if you wish it very much; but please do not circulate it, and of course that means no copy of it is to be made.* You will just have to bear with my sensitiveness. I have known one or two writers as bad as that—writers more competent, more firmly established in their craftsmanship than I. I don't think that's a sickly trait; it's just individual temperament, and I guess we'll have to bear with it.

In more than one connection, I took occasion to expound to Dr. Winkler the characteristic attitude of non-demandingness of the Principal Ones at the Farm, the exquisitely observed policy of leaving people free. My most impressive evidence on this point was the concerted silence of the bunch of you, all these years when your souls were being tried by my delinquency—your never saying anything to me, never prodding, not so much as delicately hinting, by word or act or implication. That among yourselves you discussed the matter, and with some of the non-residents who are part of the Farm group—that I take for granted. How could you *not* take up the unsolved mystery now and then? But that you could so consistently, over so long a period, wholly refrain from saying anything whatever to me—well, I found that something to boast about, to Dr. Winkler, to Mrs. Laughlin (who, as you know, is underwriting my present endeavors—in my present condition I couldn't carry on at all without the padding she is providing), and to just two others, I think, who have been involved in the recent unfoldment: Rosemary and Clara.†

I am handing you this document with all my love.

---

*Sidney McKee (1882–1971), husband of Rose McKee, was a Congregational minister and an original associate of Gould Farm.

†Rosemary Antin and Clara Antin, two of Antin's sisters.

Yes, it has been something of a labor to write all that—of course not in one session—but when I've recovered from the physical effort, I'll feel like a new man. Confession, you know—

104. To Abraham Cronbach [AJA]

Apartment 10C,
156 East 79th Street
New York 21
October 25, 1945

Dear Dr. Cronbach:

You who are so wise—and your wisdom is newly made apparent in your fine New Year's message to me, which I am only with this acknowledging—you know that destiny cannot be forced. It does not seem to be our destiny to meet again at this period. For here am I en route to Winter Park, Fla.—I leave New York on Nov. 4th, to be gone about six months; and your visit East is much too late on the calendar.

It would not be so bad, would it, if I were a better correspondent. It is my bad habit of neglecting distant friends that creates the gulf. In your case, it is only your own faithfulness that has kept a connection open through the years. I am obliged to you for that much.

"We are not lost despite our weakness" you sum up. It is a true word; though, curiously, in these latter years, when physically I have been much reduced—especially since a heart attack last June—I have been progressively more aware of strength than of weakness. Because life has brought me closer and closer to the source of strength and incorruptibility.

It is too bad we may not meet in person, but is it not better to meet in understanding, where no physical barriers hinder?

All best wishes,

105. To Abraham Cronbach [AJA]

800 Interlocken Ave.
Winter Park, Fla.
November 6, 1945

Dear Dr. Cronbach:

Your last letter of Oct. 24 must have crossed mine telling you of my then imminent departure for the South. I have been touched by your eagerness for the meeting, which fate in the end postponed again. Perhaps the meeting will take place when and where we least expect it. I stood the journey pretty well and am glad to be settled for the winter.

106. To Abraham Cronbach [AJA]   Albany, N.Y.
                                                     September 6, 1946

Dear Dr. Cronbach:

I have been laid up again since returning to Albany or you would have heard answer in reply to your note of Aug. 29.

I feel safe now in accepting your schedule. Accordingly I shall look for you on Friday about three in the afternoon, and in the evening for seven o'clock dinner. I hope we have seen the end of interferences!

My sister wanted to invite Dr. and Mrs. Wolk to dinner, but after this latest set-back I do not feel well enough to see so many guests at once. So we shall have to be content with a very quiet evening.

I am trying my best to keep in mind the fact that you and I will find each other changed beyond recognition, and you must do the same, to lessen the inevitable shock. How many years since we met?—the years that make us over into an image that was one of several latent images when we were young.

Lancaster Street is not my home. One of my sisters and a friend of hers have their home here, while I am a bird of passage under their most hospitable roof. So you see the background also is greatly changed since Scarsdale days. A meeting after so many years has some queer bumps in it—I had an experience of this sort last winter, perhaps that's why I'm so aware, and so full of warnings.

This pleasant weather of the last few days—only let it last till after your visit, to make up to you for being cheated out of a sight of the Berkshires by my flitting to Albany. I had to see the surgeon for a check-up, or I should have received you in Monterey as first planned.

                                                     Cordially,

107. To Abraham Cronbach [AJA]   868 Lancaster Street
                                              Albany 3, N.Y.
                                              October 15, 1946

Dear Dr. Cronbach:

Dear Dr. Cronbach—Dear Dr. Cronbach—Dear Dr. Cronbach:

October 15th is not the only time I started a letter to you. There were several such beginnings. The Oct. 15 sheet was pulled out of the type-writer and clipped to a letter of yours—dated Sept. 21st—with various memoranda that accumulated, of things I wanted to say to you, as the weeks went by and I remained frozen in a sort of paralysis. After a time I realized how ill I was and I went on to New York to consult my chief medical adviser. On the train I had an accident—several fractured ribs and profound shock. The time since has been spent in a nursing home. Going on five months, that is.

Now I begin to come to life and return to my friends, many of whom, like yourself, have not known what had become of me. My illness, you see, coincided with some crucial intrusions from outside—(but is anything in the world *outside* one who has identified herself with the cosmos?). My great achievement has been to maintain a relaxed state of mind and heart in face of the knowledge that the threads of my external life were dangling in the confusion of long neglect.

You, like others, have had time to be deeply hurt by my silence, the more marked, in your case, because it followed your visit to Albany. But I know you will take me back into your friendship. I know it and I recall your talk, and—yes—your face and voice, during those two little visits. And so I shall go on as if there had been no such chilling silence on my part.

It is now March 13, at the nursing home, 202 Riverside Drive, New York 25. Another era, almost, certainly another world. The interval has favored me with some advanced lessons in the meaning of life, some further revelations of the capacity of the human heart to endure suffering, some moments of overwhelming joy in increase of faith in the cosmic order. What a world to have lived in! What a world to be leaving presently, for one more glorious with the final uncovering of all mysteries!

Now let me take up your letter and the batch of memoranda. My sister Rosemary, I think, acknowledged for me your kind gift of a copy of your *Prayers for the Jewish Advance*. I read all of it soon after it came to hand, with sympathy for the author, rather than for the substance. One characteristic of this collection did warm my heart: here, I noted, was reflected a soul all love, all patience with other people's viewpoints. Of such as the author of these prayers could be built the world of peace that everybody talks about and does so little to effect. I noted that the book had appeared all of twenty-odd years earlier, still I found *you* in these simple devotional utterances, of a piece with what you showed yourself in our two visits.

I cannot tell you how I relished your unorthodox utterances—unorthodox from the accepted Jewish standpoint. I think it is there, where you have taken the widest swing from the Jewish position—(*which* Jewish position? it could be asked; but you and I understand)—it is there that I feel you nearest to me. If opportunity allowed, it would be a great satisfaction to me to start with you from that point and find how far we could in fact go together.

One of my most precious recollections of your visit is of a moment during our talk upstairs, on your second visit. It was that morning when I sensed particularly your desire to savor our old friendship, to test its foundations in the spirit. I am afraid I let myself go a little, about anthroposophy, Rudolf Steiner. I shall never forget a question that you asked: Could one accept of anthroposophy and retain one's faith in God and the efficacy of prayer? It was not so much the substance of the question, which in your case phrased the question. My heart at that moment recorded the fact that I was face to face with a man of true humility.

I studied thoughtfully the copy of the *Purpose of the Jewish Peace Fellowship*. I was—am—grateful to have this effort made clear to me. In every such endeavor of intelligent goodwill I rejoice. What you told me orally, added to this written statement, answers my question, Why a separate *Jewish* Peace Fellowship?

Whether you find any time to get acquainted with Rudolf Steiner will depend not on your external situation—how busy you are, what other interests claim your attention—but on your destiny. If your time has come to explore this modern path of initiation, nothing can keep you from it. I shall wait and watch with interest. Meanwhile, I shall carry out some minimum of my impulse to open the way for you—that being *my* destiny—by suggesting some connections. Thus, I venture to enclose with this letter the reprint of an article by a distinguished pupil of Rudolf Steiner, an anthropologist, now settled in this country. There are many other items I might choose as an introduction, but I have nothing at hand in such compact form—indeed, I have little at hand in any form, as I did not bring any books with me. What I would like to put into your hands is the *Introduction*—just that one chapter titled "The Character of Occult Science" (in the original, "Die Geheimwissenschaft im Umriss"). Very emphatically I would recommend "Turning Points in Spiritual History" (I note that the original, Wendenpunkte des Geisteslebens, is marked in the catalogue *vergriffen*). "Three Paths of the Soul to Christ" is an important short treatment. I doubt that you would find many of the originals—it is an ocean of literature I am referring to—among the group of anthroposophists in your city, but English translations you could probably borrow, and the translations of the several works I have mentioned are not bad. I did mention that there is a group in Cincinnati, I think. I find on enquiry that the leader is Mr. William Ringwald, 1437 Yarmouth Avenue, Cincinnati 29. I have no idea what sort of people you would find in this group—every sort is attracted, and some are skilful and some are inept in meeting new enquirers. When and if you are interested to seek an introduction, you will take the chance, as I am doing, on the sort of intermediary you may meet. (I have met two or three of the Cincinnati group, at summer conferences at Spring Valley, N.Y. Of these I remember only the novelist, Mrs. Stewart (can't call up the first name, but her first novel, *Let the Earth Speak,* made a great impression on me. She has written more that I have not read. Her husband also is a genial person.)

My attention has been called to a reference, in *Readers Digest* for March, by Prof. Milliken, to Lecomte du Nouy's recent book, *Human Destiny,* that is being much talked about at the moment. Milliken says that so far as he knows nobody versed in modern natural science has previously tried to re-establish God in his place. (My quotation is from memory, but you will find that I reproduce the sense of Milliken's comment.) The fact is that Rudolf Steiner, a scholar of severe scientific training, one at the same time deeply versed in the humanities, rebuilt the foundations of religious faith for our age in a lifetime of labor—as writer, lecturer, pedagogue, artist—commencing half a century ago.

March 14. —To clear the slate completely, let me tell you that I have not forgotten your several-times-repeated request for permission to donate my letters to your college library. I have so wanted to say "please don't," but was unwilling to say that without careful explanation, and never got around to formulating the explanation. By my default you win. Having so ill used you in the matter of a courteous enquiry, I cannot do other than give my consent at this late day. That sounds grudging, doesn't it? It isn't meant to be. It's a way of saying that I hope my shamefully tardy action will win for me your forgiveness. A bargain, in other words.

I remain in New York until May. Perhaps something will bring you to New York during this interval. Write to the Albany address. I am now trying to find quarters more normal and pleasant than a nursing home. A vagabond I shall remain, it is certain, to the end of my days on earth.

With best wishes,

108. To Abraham Cronbach [AJA]

Till some time in May
address 123 Waverly Place
New York 14, N.Y.
April 2, 1947

Dear friend:

Breaking all my past records, I am writing by return mail in reply to your choice letter of March 16—which has wandered about to find me at one more temporary address. I am a "homeless soul" in more than the esoteric sense.

I have not many friends who would endure the extended neglect you have been treated to not only without resentment, but with uncooled affection and patience. I begin to see that your dominant trait may be humility.

I am touched by your revelation of your youthful concept of the ministry which you still lionize today. You have come nearer bringing that concept into life than perhaps you realize. It is the priestly quality in you that forms, I think, the firmest plank in the bridge between your inner life and mine, in many respects so diverse.

I know how you feel about a suitable time to "break new intellectual ground," in respect to an introduction to Rudolf Steiner's work. I myself made an *eleven-year* detour, from my first recognition that Rudolf Steiner was a phenomenon that concerned me, to my first systematic study. I hope your destiny will allow you to avoid such a detour. We haven't so much time any more, you and I, if we are to talk over the meaning of anthroposophy in earthly language.

Do not allow yourself the notion that I am not in need of the prayers of a sincere and devout priest. If I were actually as advanced spiritually as you try to make out, I would still need your prayers to keep me from falling from grace.

April 18th I should be at the convenient Manhattan address given in this letter. Do not fail to allow time for a comfortable visit with me. I am staying with the younger of my two sisters whom you met in Albany, Clara, who is the teacher. Best wishes for the Passover season.

Gratefully,

109. To Abraham Cronbach [AJA]

As from
868 Lancaster St.
Albany 3, N.Y.
October 1, 1947

Dear Dr. Cronbach:

I missed your New Year letter and wondered whether perhaps it had gone astray in the mails. For so many years your friendship was renewed, as it were, at that season, in a message always fresh and warming.

Your last visit, at 123 Waverly Place, left a vivid impression of your aliveness of spirit. It has been altogether a good thing to know you these many years since the Scarsdale incident of which you retained such a dramatic recollection. All the good people whom you remember in connection with it seem still very near because you so remembered them.

I had a very poor summer—health very low—but just now I feel what I hope is a turning of the tide.

Always cordially yours,

110. To Abraham Cronbach [AJA]

Great Barrington, Mass.
October 10, 1947

Dear friend:

Your letter was worth waiting for. Your very soul speaks in these few lines, and in soul we are kindred even more than in thought.

I feel blessed by your inner message. "Nothing that I could report about myself is of greater consequence," you say. If one has learned anything of life—and you have learned much—one comes to a time when we recognize the external events of a personal sort as irrelevancies. Give me "news" of yourself, dear friend, always in terms of your inner life, where soul and spirit move.

Cordially yours,

Appendix
Bibliography
Index

Appendix

Letters to Mary Antin

1. From Theodore Roosevelt [LC]   April 29, 1913

My dear Mrs. Grabau:

   This is to introduce to you Mrs. Henry A. Alexander, the mother of the dear girl whom my son married, and herself one of the most charming women I know. She wishes to meet you and is deeply interested in the various public questions with which you have now become peculiarly identified.

   With hearty good wishes,

                                                         Faithfully yours,

2. From Theodore Roosevelt [LC]   [undated]

My dear Mrs. Grabau:

   On the suffrage you occupy the same position as Mrs. Roosevelt, and the same position that many of the Progressives do. I believe in women suffrage myself, but I do not think that it is of prime importance compared to a great many other matters. I want your photograph simply as I want the photograph of Jacob Riis and Jane Addams (who does not agree with me on a great many subjects); and of others who are my political foes and have always opposed me, but whom I regard as upright and honest men and women.* Most of the photographs in the book are those of friends, but several are of people who though personally friendly to me disagree with my opinions but whom I respect; and, my dear Mrs. Grabau, you are

---

   *Jane Addams (1860–1935), an author and pacifist, was a pioneer U.S. settlement worker and founder of Hull House in Chicago.

an American in whom I so deeply believe that I should be sorry if I could not include your photograph with those of Jane Addams and Miss Kellor.*

Give my regards to your husband.

Sincerely yours,

P.S. I shall at once alter what I said which makes it look as if you are an advocate of suffrage.

3. From Theodore Roosevelt [LC]   May 23, 1914

My dear Mrs. Grabau:

It is all I can do not to say, (My dear Mary Antin).

I want to thank you and your brother-in-law for the book.† I appreciate his binding it and now it will occupy, as long as I live, one of the most honored places in my library.

I cannot tell you how much help and strength you have always been to me.

Faithfully yours,

4. From Israel Zangwill [CZ]   May 29, 1914

Dear Mrs. Grabau:

Many thanks for your family greeting to me. I take the opportunity of congratulating you most heartily upon your recent pronouncement upon American ideals. I wonder if we Jews will succeed in educating the Americans in Americanism.

With kind regards to yourself and your husband,

Yours sincerely,

5. From Ruth F. Woodsmall [SS]   717 N. Tejon Street
Colorado Springs, Colo.
February 20, 1916

My dear Miss Antin:

As a group of native-born Americans, whose forefathers fought not only to establish our government but also to preserve its integrity in its most critical period, we listened to your lecture last evening with keen interest but with no little astonishment at its entirely critical tone. To a thoughtful person, it would seem that an expression of gratitude to the country which, as you admit, has given you everything might be a fitting preface to your impassioned denunciation of that country

*Frances Alice Kellor (1873–1947), a social reformer, lawyer, and sociologist, helped lead the Progressive attack on problems of the new immigrants. She wrote *Out of Work* (1915) and *Inauguration and the Future* (1920).

†Amadeus Grabau's brother John Grabau, a bookbinder, at Antin's request bound a copy of *The Promised Land* especially for Roosevelt.

in its attitude toward the immigrant. We failed to find any such expression of gratitude, and our query is, Does this feeling exist? Has not America by your own admission exemplified, as no other country on the globe, the doctrine of Liberty and Equality? Are not you yourself, in your utter freedom of speech, a perfect example of the liberty which America accords to one and all within her gates? Since, in view of all you have received, your attitude is wholly critical, what may we expect from the ordinary immigrant, who has not your native ability?

We can of course fully appreciate your plea for the immigrant. We admit that there are many deplorable conditions in our country, and that America has not yet adequately solved the problem of the immigrant. But we cannot help feeling that, in your stress upon America's duty to the immigrant, you have lost sight of the immigrant's debt of gratitude to America. Would not your criticism be much more kindly received by a tolerant American audience, and your cause more genuinely advanced if you acknowledged the honest and intelligent effort America has already made in behalf of the immigrant?

Inasmuch as America cannot now adequately handle the immigrant situation either economically or educationally, what would be your constructive policy in case of unrestricted immigration? As you deny the validity of all statistics to prove the results of immigration upon American life, on what do you base your forecast for the future, when all who knock at the gates shall be admitted?

We have written this letter not in a spirit of controversy but of intelligent inquiry, as our professions have brought us in contact with the immigrant and hence the problem is of vital interest to us. We are enclosing a stamped envelope in the sincere hope that an answer to our questions will not be too great a demand upon your time.

Very truly yours,

Bibliography

Works by Mary Antin

Books

1899. *From Plotsk to Boston*. Boston: Clark.
1912a. *The Promised Land*. Boston: Houghton Mifflin. 1997. New York: Penguin.
1914. *They Who Knock at Our Gates: A Complete Gospel of Immigration*. Boston: Houghton Mifflin.

Periodical Publications

Fiction

1911. "Malinke's Atonement." *Atlantic Monthly* 108 (Sept.): 300–319.
1913a. "The Amulet." *Atlantic Monthly* 111 (Jan.): 31–41.
1913b. "The Lie." *Atlantic Monthly* 112 (Aug.): 177–90.

Nonfiction

1912b. "First Aid to the Alien." *Outlook* 101 (June 29): 481–85.
1912c. "How I Wrote *The Promised Land*." New York *Times*. June 30, 392.
1912d. "A Woman to Her Fellow-Citizens." *Outlook* 102 (Nov. 2): 482–86.
1917. "A Confession of Faith." *Boston Jewish Advocate* (Feb. 15): 5.
1925. "His Soul Goes Marching On." Berkshire *Courier*. May 14.
1937. "The Soundless Trumpet." *Atlantic Monthly* 159 (May): 560–69.
1941. "House of One Father." *Common Ground* 1 (spring): 36–42.

Secondary Sources

Antler, Joyce. 1997. "Autobiographies of Alienation and Assimilation: Mary Antin and Anzia Yezierska." In *The Journey Home: Jewish Women and the American Century*, 17–26. New York: Free Press.

Avery, Evelyn. 1986. "Oh My 'Mishpocha'! Some Jewish Women Writers from Antin to Kaplan View the Family." *Studies in American Jewish Literature* 5: 44–53.

Badt-Strauss, Bertha. 1977. *White Fire: The Life and Works of Jessie Sampter.* New York: Arno Press.

Bates, Stuart E. 1937. *Inside Out: An Introduction to Autobiography.* New York: Sheridan House.

Bergland, Betty Ann. 1991. "Reconstructing the 'Self' in America: Patterns in Women's Autobiographies." Ph.D. diss., Univ. of Minnesota.

Chronbach, Abraham. 1959. "Autobiography." *American Jewish Archives* 3, no. 4 (Apr.): 40–43.

Cohen, Sarah Blacher. 1977. "Mary Antin's *The Promised Land:* A Breach of Promise." *Studies in American Jewish Literature* 3: 28–35.

Demirturk, Emine Lale. 1987. "The Female Identity in Cross-Cultural Perspectives: Immigrant Women's Autobiographies." Ph.D. diss., Univ. of Iowa.

Fowler, Lois J., and David H. Fowler, eds. 1990. "Mary Antin." In *Revelations of Self: American Women in Autobiography*, 159–203. New York: State Univ. of New York Press.

Glanz, Rudolph. 1976. *The Jewish Woman in America: Two Female Immigrant Generations.* New York: Ktav Publishing.

Greenberg, Abraham Herbert. 1956. "Ethnocentric Attitudes of Some Jewish American Writers." Ph.D. diss., Yeshiva Univ.

Guttmann, Allen. 1971. *The Jewish Writer in America: Assimilation and the Crisis of Identity.* New York: Oxford Univ. Press.

Handlin, Oscar. 1971. "Mary Antin." In *Notable American Women, 1607–1950: A Biographical Dictionary*, edited by Edward T. James and Janet Wilson James, 57–59. Cambridge: Harvard Univ. Press.

Juan, V. C. 1961. Introduction to *The World We Live In: A New Interpretation of Earth History*, by Amadeus Grabau. Beijing: Geological Society of China.

Koppelman, Susan. 1984. "Mary Antin." In *Dictionary of Literary Biography*, edited by Jean Ross, 225–32. Detroit: Gale Research.

Lewisohn, Ludwig. 1950–1951. "A Panorama of a Half-Century of American Jewish Literature." *Jewish Book Annual* 5711: 3–10.

McKee, Rose. 1963. *"Brother Will" and the Founding of Gould Farm.* Great Barrington, Mass.: William Gould Corp.

McKee, William J. 1991. Interview by editor. Monterey, Mass., Nov. 9.

———. 1994. *Gould Farm: A Life of Sharing.* Monterey, Mass.: William J. Gould Associates.

Oppenheim, Janet. *Shattered Nerves.* New York: Oxford Univ. Press.

Phillips, Harriet. 1991. Interview by editor. Monterey, Mass., Nov. 9.

Proefriedt, William A. 1990. "The Education of Mary Antin." *Journal of Ethnic Studies* 17 (winter): 81–100.

Ross, Anne. 1991. Interview by editor. Averill Park, N.Y., Nov. 17.

Ross, Josephine. 1991. Interview by editor. Averill Park, N.Y., Nov. 17.

Roosevelt, Theodore. 1913. "Applied Idealism: Chapter of a Possible Autobiography." *Outlook* (June).

Rubin, Steven J. 1986. "Style and Meaning in Mary Antin's *The Promised Land:* A Reevaluation." *Studies in American Jewish Literature* 5: 35–43.

———. 1988. "American Jewish Autobiography, 1912 to the Present." In *Handbook of American-Jewish Literature,* edited by Louis Freed. New York: Greenwood Press.

Seddon, Richard, ed. 1988. *Rudolph Steiner: Essential Readings.* Northamptonshire, Eng.: Aquarian Press.

Sollors, Werner. 1986. *Beyond Ethnicity: Consent and Descent in American Culture.* New York: Oxford Univ. Press.

———. 1997. Introduction to *The Promised Land,* by Mary Antin, xi–lvi. New York: Penguin.

Solomon, Barbara Miller. 1956. *Pioneers in Service: The History of Jewish Philanthropies of Boston.* Boston.

Tuerk, Richard. 1986. "The Youngest of America's Children in *The Promised Land.*" *Studies in American Jewish Literature* 5: 29–34.

Warner, Sam Bass, Jr. 1984. *Province of Reason.* Cambridge: Harvard Univ. Press.

Wasson, Kirsten Anna. 1993. "Daughters of Promise, Mothers of Revision: Three Jewish American Immigrant Writers and Cultural Inscriptions of Identity." Ph.D. diss., Univ. of Wisconsin–Madison.

Index